Saint Ignatius Loyola–
The Spiritual Writings

Selected Books in the
SkyLight Illuminations Series

Saint Ignatius Loyola—
The Spiritual Writings

Selections Annotated & Explained

Annotation by Mark Mossa, SJ

Walking Together, Finding the Way®
SKYLIGHT PATHS®
PUBLISHING
Woodstock, Vermont

Saint Ignatius Loyola—The Spiritual Writings:
Selections Annotated & Explained

2012 Quality Paperback Edition, First Printing
Annotation and introductory material © 2012 by Mark Mossa

For information regarding permission to reprint material from this book, please mail or fax your request in writing to SkyLight Paths Publishing, Permissions Department, at the address / fax number listed below, or e-mail your request to permissions@skylightpaths.com.

Grateful acknowledgment is given for permission to use excerpts from *A Pilgrim's Testament: The Memoirs of St. Ignatius of Loyola* (referred to as *Memoirs*) and *Ignatius of Loyola: Letters and Instructions* © The Institute of Jesuit Sources, St. Louis, MO. Used by permission. All rights reserved.

Library of Congress Cataloging-in-Publication Data
Ignatius, of Loyola, Saint, 1491–1556.
[Selections. English. 2012]
St. Ignatius—the spiritual writings : selections annotated & explained / annotation by Mark Mossa. — Quality pbk. ed.
p. cm. — (SkyLight illuminations)
Includes bibliographical references (p.   ) and index.
ISBN 978-1-59473-301-7 (alk. paper)
1. Spiritual life—Catholic Church. I. Mossa, Mark. II. Title. III. Title: Saint Ignatius—the spiritual writings. IV. Title: Spiritual writings.
BX4700.L7A25 2012
248—dc23
2012012131

10 9 8 7 6 5 4 3 2 1

Manufactured in the United States of America

SkyLight Paths Publishing is creating a place where people of different spiritual traditions come together for challenge and inspiration, a place where we can help each other understand the mystery that lies at the heart of our existence.

SkyLight Paths sees both believers and seekers as a community that increasingly transcends traditional boundaries of religion and denomination—people wanting to learn from each other, *walking together, finding the way.*

SkyLight Paths, "Walking Together, Finding the Way" and colophon are trademarks of LongHill Partners, Inc., registered in the U.S. Patent and Trademark Office.

Walking Together, Finding the Way®
Published by SkyLight Paths® Publishing
A Division of LongHill Partners, Inc.
Sunset Farm Offices, Route 4, P.O. Box 237
Woodstock, VT 05091
Tel: (802) 457-4000   Fax: (802) 457-4004
www.skylightpaths.com

Contents ☐

INTRODUCTION
A Practical Mysticism ☐

Inscribed on the walls of the School of Education at the University of Florida you'll find the names of those considered to be among the greatest educators in the history of Western civilization. Among them is the name "Loyola," which refers to a region in the Basque country of Spain that was the birthplace of the individual to whom it refers, Iñigo de Loyola. As he is more commonly known, Saint Ignatius of Loyola was a sixteenth-century mystic and principal founder of the Roman Catholic missionary order of priests and brothers known as the Society of Jesus, or the Jesuits. No one would appreciate the irony of being placed among such a distinguished company of teachers and educational innovators more than Ignatius himself. For while he certainly was a great innovator, he was not one with a natural inclination toward academic studies and at times even seems anti-intellectual. Though indeed the religious community that he founded went on to establish one of the largest educational networks in the world and has and continues to produce noted (some would say "notorious") teachers and scholars, this was quite far from the vision with which Ignatius began.

Ignatius saw the Jesuit mission as being to "set fire to the world," igniting a love for Christ in the hearts of all to whom Jesuits were sent. And there can be no doubt that he and his "first companions" who founded this new religious order were the spark that ignited a new and revolutionary religious movement which would do more than they ever imagined. Their initial vision was simply, explains Jesuit historian John O'Malley, "the help of souls." This focused more on the "basics"— the education of children in the faith, works of mercy, preaching, and the hearing of confessions. Yet, their numbers grew rapidly, as did their influence. Though the establishment of schools was not part of their original vision, within a decade they were being invited to do so, and eventually Ignatius believed this an indication of God's will. Jesuits also quickly became advisors, teachers, and confessors to monarchs and nobles throughout Europe, and soon, by means of their missionary endeavors, their influence would extend around the world to the furthest reaches of Asia and South America. This caused some to be suspicious of their intentions, and even to imagine diabolical conspiracy theories, which endure to this day.

One could say that Jesuits have always been a bit misunderstood. That Ignatius has attained the status of a great educator is but one example of such misunderstanding, for Ignatius's greater gifts were as an organizer and spiritual director. While as superior of the Jesuits it was he who originally allowed the schools to be established, other Jesuits developed the order's distinctive educational vision. Jesuits have been characterized throughout history as great equivocators who, being overly educated, were more apt to make generous distinctions rather than to speak the truth plainly and without qualification. Because the founding of the Jesuits took place amidst the turmoil of the Protestant Reformation, Ignatius is often painted as a great "counter-reformer." And, while it is true that early Jesuits like Peter Canisius slowed and even reversed the spread of Protestantism in places like Germany, such efforts took place amidst Ignatius's own hopes that the Society of Jesus would contribute to needed reforms within the Roman Catholic Church itself. It is perhaps telling that in his thousands of letters (he was the most prolific letter writer of his time) he spends very little time addressing or arguing points of contention between Catholics and Protestants.

Indeed, Ignatius's own convictions about the Jesuits and the church that he loved earned him as many friends as detractors among ecclesiastical authorities. For example, he promoted the frequent reception of Holy Communion when this was not the norm. He steadfastly believed that

God had given him the name for his new religious order, the Society (or more literally translated, the "company") of Jesus. Thus he stubbornly resisted all attempts by members of the church hierarchy, many of whom thought the name presumptuous, to change it to something more consistent with other orders who tended to take their names either from their founder (e.g., the Franciscans) or some special devotion (e.g., the Sacred Heart). Ignatius usually found ways to wait out those who tried to force his hand, seeing many retire or die before achieving their goal.

Meeting similar resistance was one of Ignatius's most radical innovations to religious life. All religious communities up until this point required that its members gather regularly throughout the day for communal prayer. Ignatius's vision, however, was of a community whose priority would be its ministry, ministry that would make irregular and different demands of individual members of the community. The model of Jesuit community would come to be known as one of "contemplatives in action," each priest and brother required to attend mass and engage in daily prayer, but according to a schedule dictated by his ministry rather than at mandated times. Though this innovation was affirmed in the church's official establishment of the Society of Jesus, it did not stop later church officials from imposing the more traditional prayer in common on the Jesuits for brief periods of time. Ignatius, again, would simply wait it out until he could convince subsequent authorities to reverse the decision. He was at once a steadfastly obedient servant of the church and the pope and a visionary stubbornly dedicated to the unique demands of a religious community whose spiritual practices would be focused on and shaped by the demands of their ministry instead of by traditional models of religious life.

The Making of a Saint

This brief survey of the foundations of the Society of Jesus gives us some indication as to who Ignatius became. However, to understand Ignatius's great contribution to the Christian church and the history of spirituality fully, we must go back to his beginnings, when his imaginings were focused on courtly life and wooing women, not on discerning God's will or becoming a saint. Ignatius lived the life of a courtier and soldier well into his twenties. He was known to be a capable soldier, and it was an experience of battle that changed the course of his life. Ignatius fought on the side of the Spanish in a battle against the French at Pamplona. His military unit, finding themselves seriously outnumbered, was on the verge of surrender when Ignatius, displaying his gifts for charismatic (even if, in this case, foolish) leadership, convinced his comrades to fight on. And they did, at least until Ignatius's leg was shattered by a cannonball, and their defeat seemed inevitable.

It was during Ignatius's recovery from this injury (one that brought him close to death) that a change in him began to take place. He longed to read stories of romance and chivalry while confined to his bed, but the only books available were on the lives of Christ and the saints. As Ignatius began to read the life of Saint Francis or Saint Dominic, unexpectedly he found himself longing to live his life as they did—even though he still had dreams of courtly and romantic life. Each of these imaginings would excite passion within him, for a time. He began to pay closer attention to the dynamics of these movements in his mind and heart, and soon realized that while his passion for the exploits of courtly love would fade quickly, his excitement about the possibility of being a saint tended to stay with him much longer. He soon saw in this the will of God, and his experience of arriving there would provide some of the primary insights of his *Spiritual Exercises* with regard to discernment of our life vocation. Upon his recovery, Ignatius chose not to return to the worldly life of the court, but instead to become a pilgrim, an itinerant preacher of sorts, who would travel the highways and byways, sharing his insights and engaging in spiritual conversation with others. Exchanging his clothing for that of a beggar, Ignatius gave himself over radically to God's will. At the heart of Ignatian spirituality, then, is this impulse toward conversation with God, and with others.

The Ignatian Exercises

On his pilgrim journey, Ignatius received many insights, which he began collecting in a book he called *The Spiritual Exercises*, meant to help others realize similar insights for themselves. Ignatius also spent much of his time begging, fasting, praying, and engaging in works of charity. At the beginning, he was afflicted with extreme scrupulosity, engaging in extreme penances, and often giving away the little money he had, for fear he was not trusting enough in God. Yet he also matured during this process and, with the aid of various spiritual advisors, learned to be less inclined to extreme sacrifices, especially when it threatened his already fragile health. In his autobiography he speaks of these things, and we witness the "on-the-job" training of a saint. He was gifted with mystical visions but he also soon learned that, as with his penances, such gifts could distract from the work at hand. He famously decided to forego his mystical insights for a time because they were getting in the way of completing his university courses!

Ignatius's retreat manual, *The Spiritual Exercises,* composed during the course of his pilgrimage and up through the founding of the Society of Jesus, forms the foundation of a directed retreat experience, meant ideally to take place over thirty days of silent prayer. However, knowing such a commitment would be difficult for many, Ignatius allowed for shorter variations, and even designed a form that people could follow in the midst of everyday life. The *Exercises* are meant to help a person discern God's will for his or her life. They are organized into four "weeks," focusing first on our personal relationship with God, especially our own sinfulness, then on the life of Jesus, Jesus's passion and death, and the resurrection. Most of the prayers of the *Exercises* focus on passages from scripture, or beliefs and devotions from Christian tradition.

The Spiritual Exercises, drawn as they are from Ignatius's own growth in Christian maturity and discipline, are thoroughly intertwined with his own life and his own context. Since they are written in the style of a manual for retreat directors rather than as a devotional work, Ignatius's spiritual insights are better understood in the context of his other writings. Therefore, in addition to *The Spiritual Exercises*, this book will also draw on Ignatius's spiritual autobiography as well as his wide correspondence and his instructions about the spiritual life for people from many different walks of life. By means of excerpts from these texts, and my own commentary, I hope you will enjoy learning more about Ignatius's "practical mysticism."

Ignatius's Key Concepts

All religious and spiritual traditions come with their own set of practices and vocabulary, which may seem foreign, even confusing, to the uninitiated. Ignatian and Jesuit spirituality is no exception. Indeed, for many readers there may be a dual challenge, for in this case we are dealing with a "tradition within a tradition." The spiritual tradition inspired by Ignatius exists within the larger Roman Catholic religious tradition and thus presumes certain understandings on the part of its participants and practitioners. Even then, however, Ignatius sometimes uses traditional Catholic terms like "meditation" and "contemplation" in ways that are peculiar to him. Thus, it will be helpful to take a few moments to introduce some of the key concepts that make up Ignatius's spiritual vision.

The Spiritual Exercises

The Spiritual Exercises are the foundation of Ignatian Spirituality. These exercises, however, are not a work of spiritual literature meant to be read but are meant rather as something of a "how-to" manual for the person directing another in the retreat experience it outlines. This is a silent retreat meant to take place over a period of thirty days (though making allowance for shorter versions, and a version undertaken in daily life) divided into four "weeks." These "weeks" are not of equal length and can vary in the number of days based upon the progress of the person making the retreat. Each week has a specific theme. The first week focuses on human sinfulness; the second on the life of Jesus; the third on

Jesus's betrayal, trial, and execution; and the fourth on his resurrection from the dead. These exercises offer spiritual insights, guides for prayer, and spiritual direction drawn from Ignatius's own experience of conversion as well as from the conversations he had with people while on the road. Additional instructions, insights, and options are also included in a set of twenty "annotations" to the exercises.

The First Principle and Foundation

The exercises begin with a statement by Ignatius about what he believes to be the main end of the spiritual life and the means by which that end should be achieved. He explains it in this way:

> Man is created to praise, reverence, and serve God our Lord, and by this means to save his soul. And the other things on the face of the earth are created for man and that they may help him in prosecuting the end for which he is created.
>
> From this it follows that man is to use them as much as they help him on to his end, and ought to rid himself of them so far as they hinder him as to it.
>
> For this it is necessary to make ourselves indifferent to all created things in all that is allowed to the choice of our free will and is not prohibited to it; so that, on our part, we want not health rather than sickness, riches rather than poverty, honor rather than dishonor, long rather than short life, and so in all the rest; desiring and choosing only what is most conducive for us to the end for which we are created.

Indifference

When Ignatius speaks of "indifference," he is not saying that we should cease to care about other people, ideas, our environment, or our own health. What he does mean is that these should not be allowed to get in the way of or take precedence over the one thing to which we should never be indifferent—God's love and will for us. Thus we should value all other things not for their own sake, but insofar as they contribute to uniting us more fully with God and God's will.

Sin

It is worth saying a little bit about sin because even though the word is familiar, it is of great importance in Ignatius's approach to the spiritual life. Based upon his own experience, Ignatius believed that we could not advance in the spiritual life without first contending with our own sinfulness. Thus, the first "week" of the exercises is intended primarily as a time of reflection on one's own sin, and on sin in the world. Ignatius's way of approaching sin is distinctively Catholic, and thus is understood very much in terms of Roman Catholic tradition regarding penance and confession. Ignatius encourages making a "general confession" to God of all our past sins by means of the Sacrament of Penance, which involves confessing to a priest. He also urges the examination of conscience, usually a means of preparation for confession, which helps us to review the sins we have committed since our most recent confession. But it is also worth noting that he warns repeatedly against excessive scrupulosity, especially of the kind he was guilty of in the early days of his conversion, confessing the same sins over and over rather than trusting that God had forgiven him.

Ignatius also practiced self-mortification, engaging in sacrificial and penitential acts that are aimed at making amends for our sins, encouraging greater trust in God, or teaching humility. This included such practices as fasting, begging alms, walking barefoot, neglecting one's physical appearance, and self-flagellation. Eventually, however, Ignatius reached a point where he encouraged these disciplines only to the extent that they helped someone's progress in the spiritual life. This more considered approach, as we shall see, resulted from Ignatius's recognition of the ways in which his own excessive use of such practices once jeopardized his own health and well-being.

The Examen

The examen, which Jesuits are required to do twice a day, is similar to the examination of conscience. It differs in that it examines a relatively short period of time (Ignatius recommended doing it once or twice a day), and because it serves not only as an inventory of sins committed, but also as a means of awareness and thanksgiving for gifts received during that same time period. Basically, it is a review of the day, recognizing our sins, but also the ways that God has been present in our relationships and experiences.

The Election

One of the main purposes of the spiritual exercises is toward making an "election," the choice of what would commonly be referred to today as our "vocation" or "calling." While it is clear that Ignatius saw this largely in terms of determining a person's state of life (e.g., marriage, priesthood, or religious life), we can engage in an election about any number of things, deciding to accept a job or position, or whether to undertake a religious pilgrimage of some kind, for example.

Forms of Prayer

In addition to traditional prayers like the "Our Father," and the "Hail Mary," Ignatius encourages various different ways of praying throughout the exercises. Here I will briefly describe each of them.

COLLOQUY. During certain prayer exercises, Ignatius suggests we engage in a colloquy, which means conversing with God as we would with a friend.

MEDITATION. For Ignatius, meditation means prayerful consideration of a religious mystery, event, or passage from scripture. This can take the form of considering at length one sentence or even one word from a scripture passage that you find particularly striking at the time when you are praying. The purpose of the meditation is to provide a deeper understanding of the mystery or teaching that you are meditating on, and to enable you to apply that understanding in some way to your own life.

CONTEMPLATION. Though contemplation was a long-standing Christian practice by Ignatius's time, Ignatius's view of it was unique. His approach focused on the use of the imagination in prayer, by which we insert ourselves into an event or series of events in scripture, most especially events in the life of Jesus as narrated in the four gospels. Thus Ignatius suggested contemplating events drawn from the infancy narratives, or from

Jesus's childhood and early adulthood, or from the calling of the twelve apostles, the parables, or the raising of Lazarus. This kind of contemplation not only involves being an eyewitness to the events, but participating in them directly, perhaps having a conversation with Jesus or one of the disciples by means of the imagination. Two other aspects of Ignatian contemplation are what he refers to as "composition of place" and the "application of the senses."

COMPOSITION OF PLACE. This form of prayer could stand alone, but more commonly would be the groundwork for the contemplative experience. By composing the place, you build up the environment in which you might imagine a given scene from the gospel taking place—houses, synagogues, town meeting places, the desert, the Sea of Galilee, and so on.

APPLICATION OF THE SENSES. This form of prayer is like contemplation, except that the focus is on using the imagination to experience the story in a different way, focusing on the senses: what you hear, see, smell, feel, and taste. Use of our senses not only deepens the experience of contemplation, but also by itself can reveal unexpected insights into the experience of Jesus and the apostles and how this might relate to our own lives.

ASKING FOR DESIRED "GRACES." Asking for grace is not so much a form of prayer as what Ignatius refers to as a "prelude" to prayer. Ignatius suggests that each period of prayer in which we engage begin with the request for a certain "grace." This grace is not a material thing, but usually some insight, disposition, or emotion that a person hopes to experience. In the exercises, Ignatius often offers a suggestion of a specific grace to pray for—in the third week, for example, he suggests praying for sorrow at Jesus's suffering.

Discernment of Spirits

Ignatius sees the discernment of spirits as a crucial aid to discovering God's will for our lives and offers various rules and processes to guide such discernment. Basically what it comes down to is determining whether the desires or movements of the spirit that you are experiencing originate from the "good spirit" or "evil spirit." It is likely that Ignatius would have understood such spirits as supernatural entities working in the service of God in the first case, and in the service of Satan in the other. Some people today might find such beliefs difficult, but you needn't believe in demons to recognize that some movements of the soul incline one towards God's will while others pull us away.

Ignatius places a lot of emphasis on the interior movements of *consolation* and *desolation*. Whichever of these states you are in, and the reason for being so, has important implications with regard to how, or even if you should, make important life decisions, both within and without the context of the exercises.

Consolation

Ignatius advises someone going through the exercises, as well as those who are growing in their relationship with God and discerning God's will in their daily prayer, to pay close attention to their immediate interior dispositions. Today we might describe such things in terms of our psychological state or as the experience of our affective life. Indeed, Ignatius believed that attention to our immediate desires or affections is crucial, as they have a significant affect on our spiritual progress. Thus we experience what Ignatius calls consolation when we are happy or at peace, especially when it is rooted in our affection for God and our experience of God's love. We might also find our desires are very much attuned to God's desires for us and for others. It is during such times that we are especially open to God's grace, and thus these are times when good discernment takes place and when we are able to best make decisions in response to what God wills for our lives.

Desolation

What Ignatius refers to as desolation is roughly the opposite of consolation, but must be understood in a more nuanced way than simple unhappiness or depression, though these states are certainly indications that we are experiencing desolation. A general state of lasting unhappiness, depression, unease or loneliness would be desolation, especially when such states are accompanied by a lack of spiritual desire, a sense of God's absence or, more seriously, full-blown despair. However, Ignatius would not necessarily include feelings of regret, guilt, or unworthiness as indications of desolation. Indeed, such feelings might be initially aroused precisely because our desires and affections have become more directed toward God. In that case we must look beyond our negative feelings and examine whether they stem from spiritual disaffection or from the tension between our desire to be in relationship with God and our sinful actions. Ignatius advises that if we find ourselves truly to be in a state of desolation that we refrain from making any important decisions, especially life decisions which cannot be altered. We should instead recall past experiences of consolation, with an eye to achieving consolation once again, and only then making decisions about the things we have been considering.

A Note on Language and Imagery

Ignatius uses language and imagery in his writing that reflect his background as a sixteenth-century Roman Catholic Christian as well as his upbringing as a soldier and courtier. The beginning of the founding document of the Society of Jesus, written by Ignatius, is telling in this respect: "Whoever wishes to serve as a soldier of God beneath the banner of the Cross in our Society, which we desire to be designated by the Name of Jesus, and to serve the Lord alone and the Church, his spouse, under the Roman Pontiff, the Vicar of Christ on earth, should, after a solemn vow of perpetual chastity, poverty and obedience, keep what follows in mind."

Furthermore, Ignatius calls Jesus and God by a variety of different names—Creator, Lord, King, and the Divine Majesty—and uses military imagery quite frequently, speaking of Christians (especially vowed religious) as "soldiers," gathered under the banner or standard of Christ the King and taking vows in the presence of "the entire heavenly court" (i.e., the persons of the Trinity, Mary, and the saints). As is common even among Roman Catholics today, he refers to Mary, the mother of Jesus, simply by such titles as "Our Lady" or "Blessed Mother," and the pope as simply "the Roman pontiff" or "the vicar of Christ."

Notes on the Texts

The excerpts in this volume of Saint Ignatius's spiritual writings are taken from three sources: *A Pilgrim's Testament: The Memoirs of Saint Ignatius of Loyola, The Spiritual Exercises of Saint Ignatius of Loyola,* and *Ignatius of Loyola: Letters and Instructions.* There are a few things it will be helpful to know about each text.

Ignatius dictated his memoirs to another Jesuit, Luis Goncalves da Camara, at the insistence of a number of Ignatius's Jesuit contemporaries. They are told in the third person as the story of a "pilgrim," beginning with an admission of what by then seemed a misspent youth: "Up to the age of twenty-six he was a man given to the follies of the world; and what he enjoyed most was exercise with arms, having a great and foolish desire to win fame" (*Memoirs,* 4). It is an account of the events that took place in Ignatius's life from the time of his initial conversion up until the founding of the Society of Jesus.

The Spiritual Exercises is Ignatius's most well-known work. It has guided the retreat experience of over a million Christians over the course of nearly five centuries. Its prayer exercises, annotations, and instructions to the person giving the retreat contain much spiritual wisdom. However, these are often expressed in a form meant more to be practical than conducive for spiritual reading. Thus, the excerpts, while worthwhile, will not always read as straightforward spiritual advice in the way the excerpts from his letters will. In addition, since they will sometimes lack sufficient context, getting at their spiritual significance might require some extra attention to what is being said as well as a consideration of its place in the larger context and purpose of the *Exercises.* It will also be helpful to note the observations of Jerome Nadal, one of Ignatius's companions in the founding of the Society of Jesus, at the end of Ignatius's memoirs:

> After these things had been recounted, I asked the pilgrim on October 20 about the Exercises and the Constitutions, as I wanted to know how he had drawn them up. He told me that he had not composed the Exercises all at once, but that when he noticed some things in his soul and found them useful, he thought they might also be useful to others, and so he put them in writing; for example, the examination of conscience with that arrangement of lines, etc. He told me that he derived the elections in particular from that diversity of spirit and thoughts which he had at Loyola when he was still suffering in the leg.
>
> MEMOIRS, 147

The complete collection of Ignatius's letters and instructions numbers over seven thousand, more than that of any contemporary whose collection of letters is well known. Jesuit historian John Padberg notes: "[The collection] is, for example, larger than the collected letters of Erasmus and larger than the combined collected letters of Martin Luther and John Calvin" (*Letters and Instruction,* ix). The topics and addressees vary considerably. Many are occupied with the work of the Society, addressing everything from mundane organizational issues to the problems of individual Jesuits to ways of proceeding in the work of ministry. They also include letters of congratulation and consolation, disputation, as well as both spiritual and political advice. The addressees include fellow Jesuits, benefactors, members of the church hierarchy, parents of Jesuits, noble men and women, royalty, government officials, and others who have asked for spiritual advice. Frequently, Ignatius commissioned his secretary to write the letters, which he later edited. So, sometimes the letters are not written in his own "voice." But, even if not written or even edited by Ignatius (which was the case on some occasions), they were sent with the understanding that the person writing them knew his "mind" and thus spoke authoritatively on Ignatius's behalf.

The texts of *The Spiritual Exercises* and Ignatius's memoirs are frequently cited by means of a numbering system that has become widely accepted by Ignatian scholars. Since I have written this book for those with an interest in Ignatian prayer who may be encountering Ignatius for the first time, rather than for specialists or scholars, these numbers have been omitted. The dates of Ignatius's letters have been omitted for the same reason. For those who would like to explore these texts beyond the excerpts provided in this volume, the complete text of *The Spiritual Exercises*, memoirs, and the letters can be found in the following:

> *The Spiritual Exercises of St. Ignatius: Based on Studies in the Language of the Autograph*, ed. and trans. Louis Puhl (Chicago: Loyola Press, 1968).

> *A Pilgrim's Testament: The Memoirs of St. Ignatius of Loyola*, trans. Parmananda R. Divarkar (St. Louis, MO: The Institute of Jesuit Sources, 1995).

> *Ignatius of Loyola: Letters and Instructions*, ed. Martin E. Palmer, John W. Padberg, and John L. McCarthy (St. Louis, MO: The Institute of Jesuit Sources, 2006).

Acknowledgments

To a certain extent, all Jesuits "know" the Spiritual Exercises. It's what we live and breathe, the foundation of our lives of prayer and ministry. However, some know the life and spirituality of our founder Saint Ignatius of Loyola better than others, and many better than I. Since my first exposure to Saint Ignatius and the Spiritual Exercises was still less than twenty years ago, I owe much of the knowledge and insight I share in this book to many who have been living and breathing it longer, among them two eminent scholars of the history of Ignatius and the Society of Jesus, John O'Malley, SJ, and John Padberg, SJ. I am also indebted to Billy Huete, SJ, my novice master, who guided me through the thirty days of my first experience of the "long retreat," as we call it. There, I realized the life-changing power of Ignatian spirituality, the beginning of a journey of discovery with Jesus that has become my life. I gain new insights every day from many of my Jesuit brothers, the grace of which is demonstrated by the fact that they are too numerous to mention each one individually.

I have also been blessed with the insights of my many lay friends and collaborators in retreat ministry, many of whom are as enthusiastic (if not more) about Ignatius and Ignatian spirituality as we Jesuits are. They help me to see the ways God can be found in various life experiences in which I am unable to share. Thank God for them! I am especially grateful for the many wonderful friends I've encountered in my work with Charis ministries of Chicago who, with just a few of us Jesuits in tow, are spreading the word about Ignatius in retreats for young adults all over the country! Their collective wisdom also informs this book.

And speaking of wisdom, I must thank my chief collaborators in this particular work. Nancy Fitzgerald helped me to craft the proposal, and worked with me through the initial stages of the book. Cynthia Shattuck was the first to bring the need for such a book to my attention, and became the chief editor of the book. She was the reader's greatest advocate, always after me to explain things as clearly and helpfully as possible. She was both patient and persistent, and always a great support. Emily Wichland, vice president of Editorial and Production at SkyLight Paths, shepherded the book along, ensuring its place as a worthy companion to the other fine books in the SkyLight Illuminations series. This would be a far poorer book without their dedication, determination, and encouragement.

Part 1
Ignatius
the Pilgrim

⟨∿⟩ These excerpts offer insight into the conversion process of Ignatius, which happened in the midst of his recovery from injuries sustained when a cannonball shattered his leg during a battle against the French at Pamplona, Spain. God's providence seems to be at work in that the only reading material available was that more conducive to the conversion process. Yet, it is important to take note that conversion in this case (and probably in most cases) is not a "clean break" with the past. Indeed, Ignatius finds his desire for a life of chivalry fulfilled in a more complete way as he imagines living a life like those of the saints. It is also here that we see Ignatius starting to become aware of the various interior movements and discernment of spirits that will serve as a foundation for *The Spiritual Exercises*.

1 By starting his memoirs in this way, Ignatius indicates to us one of his greatest challenges—vanity. As his memoirs progress, simply in the way he often tells the story, we also see that this was not just a challenge of his soldiering days, but that the more mature saint can at times still be impressed by his own virtue even while also being honest about his failures. This is apparent in the first part of the next excerpt, in which he portrays himself as little-bothered by a tortuous elective surgical procedure undertaken because Ignatius insisted on cutting away a protruding bone which was the result of his injuries. Rather than expressing regret for this choice, he seems proud of it.

2 Ignatius did not so much overcome his desire for a life of chivalry as replace it with something for which he found a greater and more lasting desire—becoming a saint. It also appealed to his inclination to choose that which was more "difficult and burdensome," a characteristic inclination of much of his conversion experience.

☐ Soldier or Saint?

Up to the age of twenty-six he was a man given to the follies of the world; and what he enjoyed most was exercise with arms, having a great and foolish desire to win fame.[1]

MEMOIRS, 4

After the flesh and excess bone were cut away, remedial measures were taken that the leg might not be short; ointment was often applied, and it was stretched continually with instruments that tortured him for many days. But Our Lord kept giving him health; and he felt so well that he was quite fit except that he could not stand easily on the leg and had perforce to stay in bed.

And as he was much given to reading worldly books of fiction, commonly labeled chivalry, on feeling well he asked to be given some of them to pass the time. But in that house none of those that he usually read could be found, so they gave him a Life of Christ and a book of the lives of the saints in Castilian.

MEMOIRS, 6–7

Nevertheless Our Lord assisted him, causing other thoughts, that arose from the things he read, to follow these. For in reading the life of Our Lord and of the saints, he stopped to think, reasoning with himself, 'What if I should do this which St. Francis did, and this which St. Dominic did?' Thus he pondered over many things that he found good, always proposing to himself what was difficult and burdensome and as he so proposed it, it seemed easy for him to accomplish it.[2]

MEMOIRS, 8

3 As early as the time of his convalescence, Ignatius has already begun to think about and "organize" his experience in a distinctive way, noting some "essential things" from the life of Christ so that we can see the beginnings of what would later take shape as *The Spiritual Exercises*. His description of the consolation and the desire to serve God that he experiences gazing at the sky and the stars also anticipates the final contemplation of the exercises, which suggests that contemplating God at work in nature ought to serve as an impetus to putting one's entire self at the service of God.

As he very much liked those books, the idea came to him to note down briefly some of the more essential things for the life of Christ and the saints; so he set himself very diligently to write a book (because he was now beginning to be up and about the house a bit) with red ink for the words of Christ, blue ink for those of Our Lady—on polished and lined paper, in a good hand because he was a very fine penman.

Part of the time he spent in writing and part in prayer. The greatest consolation he experienced was gazing at the sky and the stars, which he often did and for long, because he thus felt within himself a very great impulse to serve our Lord. He often thought about this intention and wished he were now wholly well so he could get on his way.[3]

MEMOIRS, 11–12

~ Despite the fact that his conversion was in some ways not a complete break with his past, Ignatius nevertheless does put a good deal of effort into starting life anew. The fact that he refers to himself in his memoirs as "the pilgrim" is one indication of this. He also leaves behind the clothes and accoutrements of his former life, dressing himself in the clothes of a beggar, and tries as much as possible not to take advantage of the privileges and connections with the nobility he formerly enjoyed because of his family name. The ideal he strives for and struggles with during his pilgrim journey is relying on God alone.

1 Ignatius's first stop on his pilgrim journey was the shrine of Our Lady of Montserrat. There he would leave his sword and spend a night in prayer before the "black Madonna" (the figures of Mary and Jesus in the statues are black), one of the most celebrated religious images in Spain, before continuing on his journey. The shrine still attracts thousands of pilgrims every year, and replicas of the black Madonna stand in many Jesuit communities as a testament to what might be seen as the very beginnings of the Society of Jesus.

2 Ignatius is indicating that this took place the evening before, often referred to as the "vigil," one of the days on the Roman Catholic calendar dedicated to a feast of Mary. This may refer to a feast peculiar to this region of Spain or, very likely, to the Feast of the Annunciation of the birth of Jesus to Mary on March 25, nine months before Christmas.

☐ The Pilgrim Sets Out

Coming to a large town before Montserrat,[1] he decided to buy there the attire he had resolved to wear—and use when going to Jerusalem. He bought cloth from which sacks are usually made, loosely woven, and very prickly. Then he ordered a long garment to be made from it, reaching to his feet. He bought a pilgrim's staff and a small gourd and put everything in front by the mule's saddle.

MEMOIRS, 23

On the eve of Our Lady in March,[2] at night, in the year 1522, he went as secretly as he could to a beggar—and stripping off all his garments he gave them to a beggar; he dressed himself in his chosen attire and went to kneel before the altar of Our Lady. At times in this way, at other times standing, with his pilgrim's staff in his hand, he spent the whole night.

MEMOIRS, 24–25

As he was gone about a league from Montserrat, a man who had been hurrying after him, caught up and asked if he had given some clothes to a beggar, as the beggar affirmed. Answering that he had, tears flowed from his eyes in compassion for the beggar to whom he had given the clothing—in compassion, for he realized they were harassing him, thinking he had stolen them.

MEMOIRS, 25

3 Ignatius often speaks forcefully in his letters about the dangers of scrupulosity, and this passage provides some insight into his concern. Early in his pilgrim journey, he became so distraught over his past sins that even though he had already confessed them, he considered taking his own life. Overcoming his distress, Ignatius attributed both the temptation to take his own life as well as the urge to confess repeatedly to the work of the evil spirit.

4 This excerpt and the one that follows illustrate one of the issues that comes up repeatedly for Ignatius during this time. Despite his fragile health, Ignatius often denied himself even ordinary comforts and pushed himself too hard out of hope for spiritual benefit. After seriously jeopardizing his health as a result on more than one occasion, he realized the need to temper such practices, even if it meant missing out on some spiritual consolations. This theme will come up repeatedly throughout his writings.

5 After his recovery, Ignatius spent about ten months of the early part of his conversion experience living in a cave just outside the town of Manresa, where he devoted himself to prayer and worked in a hospice. It was during his time in Manresa that he first began to collect some of the observations that would become *The Spiritual Exercises*. Because Ignatius's experiences at Manresa and Montserrat were so important, their names have been given to a number of Jesuit institutions and works, most commonly to Jesuit retreat centers.

But on the third day, which was Tuesday, while at prayer he began to remember his sins; and so, as in a process of threading, he went on thinking of sin after sin from his past and felt he was obliged to confess them again. But after these thoughts, disgust for the life he led came over him, with impulses to give it up.

In this way the Lord deigned that he awake as from sleep. As he now had some experience of the diversity of spirits from the lessons God had given him, he began to examine the means by which that spirit had come. He thus decided with great lucidity not to confess anything from the past anymore; and so from that day forward he remained free of those scruples and held it for certain that Our Lord had mercifully deigned to deliver him.[3]

Memoirs, 37–38

Besides his seven hours of prayer he busied himself helping in spiritual matters certain souls who came there looking for him. All the rest of the day he spent thinking about the things of God that he had meditated upon or read that day. But when he went to bed, great enlightenment, great spiritual consolations, often came to him; so that they made him lose much of the time he had allotted to sleep, which was not much. Examining this several times, he thought to himself that he had ample time assigned for converse with God, and all the rest of the day as well; and he began to doubt, therefore, whether that enlightenment came from a good spirit. He concluded that it would be better to ignore it and to sleep for the allotted time. And so he did.[4]

Memoirs, 38

At Manresa[5] too, where he stayed almost a year, after he began to be consoled by God, and saw the fruit which he bore in dealing with souls, he gave up those extremes he had formerly practiced, and he now cut his nails and his hair.

Memoirs, 41

6 Manresa lies on the Cardoner River, where Ignatius experienced the sense of enlightenment that he describes here. Ignatius always counted this experience as one of the most important of his life.

7 This is Ignatius's rather sketchy account of perhaps the most important mystical experience of his life. Though he has trouble describing it, it is a moment of clarity and understanding that changed the way he saw things for the remainder of his life. Ignatius attributed many of his insights into the dynamics of our relationship with God to this revelatory moment. Though he could not yet be certain what his future would hold, this seems to be Ignatius's "point of no return," at least in terms of his decision to devote the rest of his life to God's service.

Once he was going out of devotion to a church situated a little more than a mile from Manresa; I believe it is called St. Paul's and the road goes by the river.[6] As he went along occupied with his devotions, he sat down for a little while with his face toward the river, which ran down below. While he was seated there, the eyes of his understanding began to be opened; not that he saw any vision, but he understood and learned many things, both spiritual matters and matters of faith and of scholarship and this with so great an enlightenment that everything seemed new to him.

The details that he understood then, though there were many, cannot be stated, but only that he experienced a great clarity in his understanding. This was such that in the whole course of his life, after completing sixty-two years, even if he gathered up all the various helps he may have had from God and all the various things he has known, even adding them all together, he does not think he had got as much as at that one time.[7]

MEMOIRS, 42–43

$\sim$ The city of Jerusalem figures prominently in Ignatius's early pilgrim journey. Initially, Ignatius thought that God was calling him to Jerusalem to engage in the work of evangelizing non-Christians there. As we shall see, he did succeed in getting to Jerusalem, only to be forced to return home. Yet, despite this failure, Ignatius long remained convinced that his future, and the future of those who would become his later companions, lay in taking up their ministry there.

1 The text of the memoirs does not make clear to whom Ignatius is referring. He speaks of numerous women who cared for him during his time of illness at Manresa. He may be referring to Agnes Pascual, one of his first benefactors, and the recipient of some of his earliest extant letters. Her support, and that of others, proved especially important when he decided to continue his studies at the University of Paris.

2 This desire to be "placed with the Son," as he often described it, becomes one of Ignatius's enduring preoccupations and underlines the centrality of Jesus in his spiritual vision.

3 Pope Adrian VI, who as a younger man had been tutor to the future Emperor Charles V (the emperor when Adrian was elected), served as pope for eighteen months, from his election in 1522 until his death in 1523.

☐ Destination: Jerusalem

So he embarked, having been in Barcelona a little more than twenty days. While he was still in Barcelona before embarking, he sought out, as was his practice, all spiritual persons, even though they lived in hermitages far from the city, to converse with them. But neither in Barcelona nor in Manresa during the whole time he was there did he find persons who could help him as much as he wished; only in Manresa that woman[1] mentioned above, who told him she prayed God that Jesus Christ might appear to him:[2] she alone seemed to enter more deeply into spiritual matters. Therefore, after leaving Barcelona, he completely lost his eagerness to seek out spiritual persons.

MEMOIRS, 49

Here all who spoke to him, on discovering that he did not carry any money for Jerusalem, began to dissuade him from making that trip, asserting with many arguments that it was impossible to find passage without money. But he had great assurance in his soul and he could not doubt but that he would in fact find a way to go to Jerusalem. After receiving the blessing of Pope Adrian VI,[3] he set out for Venice eight or nine days after Easter. He did have six or seven ducats which had been given him for the passage from Venice to Jerusalem; he had accepted them, being somewhat overcome by the fears suggested to him that he would not otherwise make the passage. But two days after leaving Rome, he began to realize that this was a lack of trust on his part, and it greatly bothered him that he had accepted the ducats, so he wondered

(continued on page 15)

[4] Ignatius's reluctance to reveal his desire to help souls seems an attempt both to curb his vanity and to avoid being perceived as presumptuous in the eyes of others. Here he also seems concerned that revealing it now would result in the disapproval of others, or cause them to be suspicious of him.

[5] "Provincial" is the term used in many religious orders, including the Jesuits, to refer to the superior of all members in a given geographical area. Large religious communities like the Jesuits and Franciscans are organized and governed by means of numerous geographical "provinces" throughout the world. The superior, or leader, of each province is known as the provincial.

[6] Ignatius was resolved to remain in the Holy Land and was so sure that this was God's will that only the threat of excommunication was able to persuade him to leave. This demonstrates how seriously he took both God's will and the authority of the church hierarchy. Ignatius would not have seen this as an instance of shortsighted church authorities interfering with God's will, but rather as an indication that he had somehow misperceived it.

if it would be good to be rid of them. He finally decided to give them generously to those who approached him, who were beggars usually. He so managed that when he eventually arrived in Venice, he had no more than a small amount which he required that night.

MEMOIRS, 55–56

His firm intention was to remain in Jerusalem, continually visiting those holy places; and in addition to this devotion, he also planned to help souls. For this purpose he had brought some letters of recommendation for the Guardian and gave them to him. He told him of his intention to remain there because of his devotion; but not the second part, about wanting to help souls,[4] because he had not told this to anyone, whilst he had frequently made public the first. The Guardian answered that he did not see how he could stay because the house was in such need that it could not support the friars; for that reason, he had decided to send some with the pilgrims, to these parts. The pilgrim replied that he wanted nothing from the house, except only that when he came sometimes to confess, they would hear his confession.

MEMOIRS, 60–61

[Ignatius] replied to this that he was very firm in his purpose and was resolved that on no account would he fail to carry it out. He frankly gave them to understand that even though the Provincial[5] thought otherwise, if there was nothing binding him under sin, he would not abandon his intention out of any fear. To this the Provincial replied that they had authority from the Apostolic See to have anyone leave the place, or remain there, as they judged, and to excommunicate anyone who was unwilling to obey them; and that in this case they thought that he should not remain.[6]

MEMOIRS, 62

〰 Though Ignatius did not think the door to Jerusalem permanently closed to him, his experience there made clear to him that he would be forced to wait for some years before being able to return again. During this period of waiting, Ignatius stepped up in earnest his efforts to help souls. He also saw this time as an invitation from God to engage in studies. University life provided him a ready supply of souls to help but also drew more attention to his efforts. The infamous Spanish Inquisition, in fact, detained, imprisoned, and questioned him and his emerging group of companions on more than one occasion during this time. The Inquisition, though largely concerned with pursuing and sometimes executing those accused of heresy, also concerned themselves with religious groups and movements with origins outside the church. One such group was the "*alumbrados*," who promoted an overly spiritual practice of the Christian life that judged worship and the sacraments to be unnecessary. Because of Ignatius's emphasis on spiritual matters, he and his companions were suspected of being *alumbrados*.

1 Isabel Roser of Barcelona was one of Ignatius's earliest benefactors. After her husband's death, she got more involved with the work of the Society of Jesus and even tried unsuccessfully to found a women's religious order under Ignatius's direction.

2 Ignatius didn't have sufficient education to begin university studies immediately, so with the help of these two benefactors he spent two years doing remedial studies before moving on to the liberal arts. He even spent a period studying basics of grammar with a class of young children.

3 During this period, the liberal arts that one would study consisted largely of topics in philosophy, with an increasing emphasis on disputation and rhetoric.

4 Though clearly not certain of the exact timing, Ignatius is conscious that it was around this time that a circle of companions, like those with whom he founded the Society of Jesus, began to spend increasing amounts of time with him, engaged in similar educational, spiritual, and charitable pursuits.

☐ Suspicions and Arrests

After the pilgrim realized that it was God's will that he not stay in Jerusalem, he continually pondered in himself what he ought to do; and eventually he was rather inclined to study for some time so he would be able to help souls, and he decided to go to Barcelona.

MEMOIRS, 70–71

When he arrived at Barcelona he made his wish to study known to Isabel Roser[1] and to a Master Ardévol who taught grammar. To both this seemed a very good idea; he offered to teach him for nothing, and she to give him what he needed to support himself.[2]

MEMOIRS, 79

After two years of studying during which, so they said, he had made great progress, his master informed him he could now study the liberal arts[3] and should go to Alcalá. Even so, he had himself examined by a doctor of theology who gave him the same advice. So he set out alone for Alcalá: though he already had some companions, I think.[4]

MEMOIRS, 81

5   The University of Alcalá was founded in 1499 in hopes of helping to initiate a new golden age in Spain. In many ways it was modeled on some of the prominent universities of the day, like the University of Paris, but its founders were also determined to be innovative, incorporating elements of the emerging Christian Humanism movement led by such figures as Erasmus and Thomas More.

6   Domingo de Soto, a professor of logic at Alcalá, was making significant contributions to the field at this time. The Albert referred to here is probably the thirteenth-century German Dominican Albertus Magnus, known for his contributions to philosophy, theology, and science. Both a priest and bishop, he is among the saints of the Roman Catholic Church. The "Sentences" referred to are the writings of the twelfth-century theologian Peter Lombard, one of the first works to combine excerpts from scripture and writings of the early church theologians together with commentary. Because the "Sentences" was considered one of the most important theological works of the time, and would be well known to most university-educated people, Ignatius has no doubt that his reader will know who "the Master of the Sentences" refers to.

7   While a beginner in the liberal arts, Ignatius was observed to have a deeper knowledge and experience of things spiritual, as well as insights into Christian doctrine. This inspired some to become students of Ignatius, but also roused suspicion, especially among church authorities who feared he might be teaching erroneous or heretical things. They seemed especially wary of the fact that he made his claims with no formal authority or training.

He studied at Alcalá[5] almost a year and a half. Since he had arrived in Barcelona in the year '24 during Lent, and had studies there for two years, it was in the year '26 that he reached Alcalá. He studied the logic of Soto, the physics of Albert and the Master of the Sentences.[6] While at Alcalá, he was engaged in giving spiritual exercises and teaching Christian doctrine, and this bore fruit for the glory of God. There were many persons who came to a deep understanding and relish of spiritual things; but others had various temptations—there was one such who wanted to take the discipline but could not do so, as though the hand were held, and other similar cases. These gave rise to talk among the people, especially because of the great crowd that gathered whenever he was explaining doctrine.[7]

MEMOIRS, 82

8   These women were a mother and daughter who had made significant spiritual progress under Ignatius's direction. Despite Ignatius's dissuasion out of fear for their safety, they set out on their own on a pilgrimage. Ignatius was blamed for their absence and held prisoner until their return.

9   Ignatius and his companions had taken to wearing a garment resembling a religious habit.

10   This is something that Ignatius and his companions suffered repeatedly during the years leading up to the founding of the Society of Jesus: suspicious authorities question and even imprison them, fail to find them guilty of any serious crime or error, but nevertheless put restrictions on what they can do and teach and even wear until they have completed their studies. As he did in Jerusalem, Ignatius complies with the orders of church authorities, even while expressing his dissatisfaction with the obstacles being placed in the way of his ministry.

From the day the pilgrim entered jail until they let him out, forty-two days passed. At the end of that time, as the two pious women[8] returned, the notary came to the jail to read the sentence: he should go free; and they should dress like the other students,[9] and should not speak about matters of faith until they had studied for four more years, because they had no education. For in truth, the pilgrim was the one who had the most, and that was with little foundation. This was the first thing he used to say whenever they examined him.

MEMOIRS, 88–89

After twenty-two days of imprisonment, they were summoned to hear the sentence, which was that no error was found in their life or teaching. Therefore they could do what they had been doing, teaching doctrine and speaking about the things of God, so long as they never defined: this is a mortal sin or this is venial, until they had spent four years in further studies. After the sentence was read, the judges displayed great affection, apparently wishing to make it acceptable. The pilgrim said he would do everything the sentence ordered, but he did not find it acceptable, because without condemning him for anything they shut his mouth so he might not help his neighbor in what he could.[10]

MEMOIRS, 102–103

The University of Paris was founded in the twelfth century and is one of Europe's oldest universities. Today it is composed of thirteen independent universities, sometimes referred to collectively as the Sorbonne. It was in Paris that the idea of the formation of the Society of Jesus really took root; there Ignatius met most of the men with whom he would found the Society of Jesus and also had access to one of the most prominent theological faculties in Europe. After a final failed attempt to travel to Jerusalem, Ignatius and his companions decided to become priests and place themselves at the disposal of the pope. The question remained whether they would do so individually or as a group. After some deliberation, they chose to form a community, with Ignatius as their head, and sought papal approval.

1 After his imprisonment in Alcalá, Ignatius and his companions chose to travel to and continue their studies in Salamanca. However, he was not long in Salamanca when he was again imprisoned and questioned by representatives of the Inquisition.

2 Hoping to free himself and his companions to pursue their primary goal of "helping souls," Ignatius decided they should move to the University of Paris to complete their studies. This would help them to escape further persecution by the Spanish Inquisition and provide them with theological training beyond reproach.

3 Despite his good intentions, there is a recklessness in Ignatius's many "spiritual contacts," which probably refers to the men and women whom he guided through the exercises and gave spiritual counsel. In accounts like these he seems at times indifferent or insufficiently aware of the possible repercussions of influencing the actions of others, especially the more prominent. As with the mother and daughter previously mentioned, Ignatius would realize the need at times to temper their enthusiasm and his own so as not to cause disruption or scandal. The success of the early Jesuits' ministry to both the lower and privileged classes seems to owe something to the wisdom gained from these experiences.

☐ At the University of Paris

Now, at the time of his imprisonment in Salamanca,[1] he still felt the same desire he had to help souls, and for that reason to study first and to gather some others with the same idea, and to keep those he had.[2] Determined to go to Paris, he arranged with these that they would wait there while he went, to see if he could find some means by which they might study.

MEMOIRS, 104

The first time he returned from Flanders he got more involved than usual in spiritual contacts,[3] and he gave exercises almost simultaneously to three persons, namely, Peralta, the bachelor Castro who was at the Sorbonne, and a Vizcayan named Amador, who was at St. Barbara. These were quite transformed and so gave all they had to the poor, even their books, and began to beg alms through Paris. They went to lodge in the hospice of St. James, where the pilgrim had stayed before but which he had now left for the reasons mentioned above.

This caused great commotion in the university, for the first two were distinguished persons and well known.

MEMOIRS, 111–112

4   Also referred to in this text by his non-Anglicized name, Pierre Favre.

5   Peter Faber and Francis Xavier were among Ignatius's closest friends at the University of Paris. Faber was Ignatius's first stable companion, and the first to become a priest. Xavier found Ignatius's way attractive, but was also drawn away by his own personal ambitions. Ignatius famously challenged Xavier with Jesus's words from the Gospel of Mark: "What good is it for a man to gain the whole world, yet forfeit his soul?" (Mark 8:36, NIV). Both men joined Ignatius in the founding of the Society of Jesus. Francis Xavier was eventually sent as a missionary to Asia. A saint of the Roman Catholic Church, he is also considered one of its greatest missionaries. Faber would later be chosen as a theological advisor to the Council of Trent.

6   Ignatius's encounter with Hoces demonstrates that the move to France did not totally allay the Inquisition's suspicions. Indeed, despite the Society's becoming more prudent in their work of helping souls, there was an inherent recklessness that could not be avoided, due to the sometimes radical nature of conversion.

7   Out of devotion to the Eucharist, and a desire to progress further in the spiritual life, Ignatius waited a year to say his first mass.

8   This "change of soul" is a key moment in Ignatius's spiritual journey. It is the experience which he has desired for so long, and this assurance of being "placed with the Son" goes a long way toward explaining why, despite the opposition of some within the church, that he insisted that his newly formed community be named the "companions" or, more formally, the Society of Jesus.

9   This rather enigmatic statement seems to refer to Ignatius's growing conviction that the Jesuit mission of helping souls would inevitably and always meet with the kind of misunderstandings, suspicion, and persecution that it already had. Indeed, Ignatius urges Jesuits and all those making the course of spiritual exercises not only to expect resistance and persecution, but to pray for it.

At this time he associated with Master Peter Faber[4] and Master Francis Xavier,[5] both of whom he later won for God's service by means of the Exercises.

MEMOIRS, 118

There was also another Spaniard there called the bachelor Hoces, who was in close touch with the pilgrim and also with the bishop of Cette. Although he had some desire to make the Exercises, still he did not put it into execution.

At last he decided to begin making them. And having made them for three or four days, he spoke his mind to the pilgrim, telling him that because of the things someone had told him, he had been afraid that he would be taught some evil doctrine in the Exercises. For this reason he had brought with him certain books so he could have recourse to them, if perchance he tried to deceive him. He was helped very much by the Exercises and in the end resolved to live the pilgrim's way.[6]

MEMOIRS, 135–136

They went to Rome divided into three or four groups, the pilgrim with Faber and Laínez. On this journey he was visited very especially by God.

He had decided to spend a year without saying Mass after he became a priest,[7] preparing himself and praying Our Lady to deign to place him with her Son. One day, a few miles before reaching Rome, he was at prayer in a church and experienced such a change in his soul and saw so clearly that God the Father placed him with Christ his Son that he would not dare doubt it—that God the Father had placed him with his Son.[8]

Then on arriving in Rome he told the companions that he saw the windows were closed, meaning to say that they would have to meet many contradictions.[9]

MEMOIRS, 139–140

Part 2
The Spiritual
Exercises

1 *The Spiritual Exercises* begins with twenty annotations that describe their nature and purpose and provide insights and advice for those directing and those making the retreat. They also include a few suggestions for alternative ways to administer and lead the exercises.

2 Though Ignatius defines it in his own way, the term "spiritual exercises" is not unique to him. Various collections of such exercises had been offered before. A popular work called *The Book of Spiritual Exercises* by the Benedictine abbot Garcia de Cisneros is a manual that Ignatius is known to have read, and it is thought to have had some influence on his own exercises.

3 Though filled with interesting insights, *The Spiritual Exercises* is not exactly a book of spirituality. It is better understood as a "how-to" book or manual for a retreat director, as well as a guide for the person making the retreat. In other words, these exercises are meant to be *done*, not merely *read*. Just as physical exercise makes for a healthy body and prepares you for a physical test (think of training for a marathon, perhaps) that you are undertaking, so the course of Ignatian exercises are meant to prepare you to choose the life to which God is calling you. Nevertheless, Ignatius's approach to the spiritual life cannot be understood without reference to many of the spiritual insights it contains.

☐ Their Purpose and Goal

First Annotation[1]

By this name of Spiritual Exercises[2] is meant every way of examining one's conscience, of meditating, of contemplating, of praying vocally and mentally, and of performing other spiritual actions, as will be said later. For as strolling, walking and running are bodily exercises, so every way of preparing and disposing the soul to rid itself of all the disordered tendencies, and, after it is rid, to seek and find the Divine Will as to the management of one's life for the salvation of the soul, is called a Spiritual Exercise.[3]

THE SPIRITUAL EXERCISES

1 The first week is dedicated to the contemplation of our sins. Doing so for a "week" will hardly seem appealing. However, Ignatius wanted the first week to be a means of freeing ourselves from the obstacles of our own sinfulness, doing so also with an increased awareness of God's love for us, so that we might more freely enter into the conversation with God that the exercises are meant to facilitate.

2 The second week focuses largely on what is sometimes referred to as the "public life" of Jesus. While it also includes the less "public" events of his birth and childhood, it mainly involves the life and ministry of Jesus from the time of his temptation and baptism up until just before the Last Supper. This includes the calling of the disciples, Jesus's acts of healing, his encounters with church authorities as well as tax collectors and sinners, and his preaching and parables.

3 The third week leads us to reflect on Jesus's passion—the Last Supper with his disciples, his betrayal, and his death upon the cross.

4 The fourth and final week is focused on Jesus's resurrection from the dead and his appearances to the disciples.

5 There exists a shorter form of the exercises known as "The Exercises in Daily Life" or simply "The Nineteenth Annotation" retreat. Ignatius offered this as an option because he knew that there were many people who could benefit from the retreat who might not be free to put aside the days necessary to make the retreat. Many people today do this version of the retreat, which requires taking time for extended prayer each day and meeting with a retreat director once a week for approximately thirty weeks.

6 The Nineteenth Annotation retreat follows the same pattern as the more traditional form. The first portion of the retreat involves prayer about sin, one's own and the sin in the world. The rest of the retreat, divided into three parts, involves praying through the life of Jesus, his passion and death, and the resurrection.

☐ How Do the Exercises Work?

Fourth Annotation

The following Exercises are divided into four parts:

First, the consideration and contemplation on the sins;[1]

Second, the life of Christ our Lord up to Palm Sunday inclusively;[2]

Third, the Passion of Christ our Lord;[3]

Fourth, the Resurrection and Ascension, with the three Methods of Prayer.[4]

Though four weeks, to correspond to this division, are spent in the Exercises, it is not to be understood that each Week has, of necessity, seven or eight days. For, as it happens that in the First Week some are slower to find what they seek—namely, contrition, sorrow and tears for their sins—and in the same way some are more diligent than others, and more acted on or tried by different spirits; it is necessary sometimes to shorten the Week, and at other times to lengthen it.

THE SPIRITUAL EXERCISES

Nineteenth Annotation[5]

A person of education or ability who is taken up with public affairs or suitable business, may take an hour and a half daily to exercise himself. Let the end for which man is created be explained to him ... Let him, during three days every morning, for the space of an hour, make the meditation on the First, Second and Third Sins ... For the mysteries of Christ our Lord, let the same course be kept, as is explained below and in full in the Exercises themselves.[6]

THE SPIRITUAL EXERCISES

1 This is what Ignatius means when he speaks of "the end" for which we are created. This is the "foundation," in the context of which we are meant to discover God's unique will for ourselves. Ignatius's use of "man" here and elsewhere reflects the particular practice and prejudices of both his time and the time of this particular translation and should be understood to include both men and women.

2 The word "indifference" is often understood to mean not caring about something or someone. For Ignatius, however, "indifference" means that we should care for one thing above everything else—our relationship with God. It is only in terms of our desire to live with God forever and God's desire for us that we should be "indifferent" to all other things. This is important to understand so as not to interpret Ignatius as encouraging us to see things and other people merely as a means to an end, to be used and discarded as necessary. That is not what he is saying.

3 During the first week, a characteristic element of Ignatian prayer is introduced—the "colloquy." It describes a conversation or dialogue in prayer with God, a specific person of the Trinity (the Father, Jesus, or the Spirit), or one of the saints (most often Mary, the mother of Jesus). Ignatius adds, "The Colloquy is made, properly speaking, as one friend speaks to another, or as a servant to his master; now asking some grace, now blaming oneself for some misdeed, now communicating one's affairs, and asking advice in them."

4 At various stages of Ignatius's prayer exercises, he suggests a prayer the retreatant would know by heart, such as the "Lord's Prayer" or the "Hail Mary." Here he suggests one of his favorite prayers, the *Anima Christi*:

Soul of Christ, sanctify me; Body of Christ, save me; Blood of Christ, inebriate me; Water from the Side of Christ, wash me; Passion of Christ, strengthen me. O Good Jesus hear me, within your wounds hide me; Suffer me not to be separated from thee; From the malignant enemy defend me; At the hour of my death, call me and bid me come to thee, that with your saints I may praise thee. Forever and ever, Amen.

☐ The First Week

Principle and Foundation

Man is created to praise, reverence, and serve God our Lord, and by this means to save his soul.[1] And the other things on the face of the earth are created for man and that they may help him in prosecuting the end for which he is created.

From this it follows that man is to use them as much as they help him on to his end, and ought to rid himself of them so far as they hinder him as to it.

For this it is necessary to make ourselves indifferent[2] to all created things in all that is allowed to the choice of our free will and is not prohibited to it; so that, on our part, we want not health rather than sickness, riches rather than poverty, honor rather than dishonor, long rather than short life, and so in all the rest; desiring and choosing only what is most conducive for us to the end for which we are created.

THE SPIRITUAL EXERCISES

The Colloquy, or Conversation[3]

First Colloquy. The first Colloquy to Our Lady, that she may get me grace from Her Son and Lord for three things: first, that I may feel an interior knowledge of my sins, and hatred of them; second, that I may feel the disorder of my actions, so that, hating them, I may correct myself and put myself in order; third, to ask knowledge of the world, in order that, hating it, I may put away from me worldly and vain things. And with that a "Hail Mary."

Second Colloquy. The second: The same to the Son, begging Him to get it for me from the Father. And with that the "Soul of Christ."[4]

THE SPIRITUAL EXERCISES

5 This colloquy immediately precedes the second week of the Ignatian exercises, which focuses on Jesus's life and ministry. These questions help to put us in the mind-set of the disciples following Jesus.

6 To take full advantage of and benefit from these questions, Ignatius suggests that we ask them in the context of our awareness of how Jesus has gone to his death "for me," as a prayer for the grace of the third week also reminds us. Thus it is not just a prayer seeking God's will, or offering our obedience, but one that is meant to be motivated by gratitude for what Jesus has done for us. It is an expression of desire as much as a submission of one's will. It is also an opportunity for more intimate conversation in the context of the entirety of his human life up to the cross.

7 Throughout *The Spiritual Exercises*, Ignatius strives to help us balance the dual relationship with Jesus who is "the Divine Majesty" nailed to the cross, and the Jesus whom we are also encouraged to speak to as a friend and intimate.

Colloquy before Jesus on the Cross

Imagining Christ our Lord present and placed on the Cross, let me make a Colloquy,[5] how from Creator He is come to making Himself man, and from life eternal is come to temporal death, and so to die for my sins.

Likewise, looking at myself, [ask]:

What I have done for Christ? What I am doing for Christ? What I ought to do for Christ?[6]

And so, seeing Him such, and so nailed on the Cross, to go over that which will present itself.

The Colloquy is made, properly speaking, as one friend speaks to another, or as a servant to his master; now asking some grace, now blaming oneself for some misdeed, now communicating one's affairs, and asking advice in them.[7]

THE SPIRITUAL EXERCISES

~ Only the beginning portion of the Second Week will be presented here. A significant portion of the rest of the Second Week can be found in part 7.

~ When Ignatius speaks of "contemplation" or "contemplative prayer," he means something very specific, and a practice that differs from what is usually understood as contemplation in the monastic tradition. For Ignatius it refers to a form of imaginative prayer in which one imagines a story from Christian tradition—here, Father, Son, and Holy Spirit enthroned in the heavens—or an incident from the life of Jesus, such as the feeding of the five thousand. When we are practicing this kind of contemplation, we may place ourselves in the scene as an observer who is merely watching the action, but we are encouraged to do even more than that. We can participate as a "player" in the drama that is unfolding, imagining ourselves as one of Jesus's disciples, or as someone who is being healed or taught by Jesus.

1 Ignatius refers here to the doctrine of the incarnation, which holds that God was conceived in human form as Jesus in the womb of his mother, Mary, taking on a human body and nature, while still remaining God. Christians celebrate the birth of Jesus, at once fully human and fully divine, at Christmas.

~ Ignatius invites us here to imagine how the Trinity of three persons in one God might be involved in saving the human race. It can be quite difficult to move beyond the abstract when it comes to imagining the Trinity. No image of the Trinity is perfect. The popular image of the shamrock, three leaves in one clover, for example, seeks to capture the Trinity's "three-in-oneness" but fails to communicate its personal and intimate nature. Ignatius's image stresses the latter, focusing on the distinct persons, Father, Son, and Holy Spirit, inviting us to imagine distinct persons deliberating over the future of the human race, and their role in saving it. The aim here is not to express or understand the doctrine of the Trinity fully, but to offer us a means of using our imagination to enter into a spiritual reality we cannot fully comprehend.

☐ The Second Week

Contemplation on the Incarnation[1]

First Point. The first Point is, to see the various persons: and first those on the surface of the earth, in such variety, in dress as in actions: some white and others black; some in peace and others in war; some weeping and others laughing; some well, others ill; some being born and others dying, etc.

2. To see and consider the Three Divine Persons, as on their royal throne or seat of Their Divine Majesty, how they look on all the surface and circuit of the earth....

3. To see Our Lady, and the Angel who is saluting her, and to reflect in order to get profit from such a sight.

Second Point. The second, to hear what the persons on the face of the earth are saying, that is, how they are talking with one another, how they swear and blaspheme, etc.; and likewise what the Divine Persons are saying, that is: "Let Us work the redemption of the Human race," etc.; and then what the Angel and Our Lady are saying; and to reflect then so as to draw profit from their words.

Third Point. The third, to look then at what the persons on the face of the earth are doing ... likewise what the Divine Persons are doing, namely, working out the most holy Incarnation, etc.; and likewise what the Angel and Our Lady are doing, namely, the Angel doing his duty as ambassador, and Our Lady humbling herself and giving thanks to the Divine Majesty; and then to reflect in order to draw some profit from each of these things.

THE SPIRITUAL EXERCISES

1 This is a companion to Ignatius's contemplation on Jesus's incarnation, picking up where that left off. As such, you might simply pray the two separately, pray the two and follow that with a third, combined contemplation, or you might just combine the two from the very start, according to how you are moved. In either case, the two together signal a key moment in the exercises, providing a bridge between those contemplations that involve imagining things not contained explicitly in scripture, and those that refer to specific scriptural accounts.

〜 In this sort of contemplation, in which it would be unusual to imagine anyone present at this event besides the angel Gabriel and Mary, you might more likely imagine yourself as an outside observer rather than a participant in the scene. Since this is a contemplation based on a scriptural text, you would use the passage (provided earlier) as a starting point but would use your imagination to "fill in the blanks," so to speak. Since this event is one of the most commonly depicted events in the art of the last two thousand years, one or several of these depictions might also be used as an aid to your imagination.

2 In this meditation Ignatius is describing what he calls the "composition of place." Its purpose is to imagine ourselves in a particular place, often the place where we imagine we would meet Jesus (usually a gospel story), that will be conducive to our prayer experience, that will make it more "real." The composition of place helps move it beyond just being a story, inviting you to get a sense of the space in which things are taking place—a building, a village square, a grassy field.

3 One of the most important elements of prayer in *The Spiritual Exercises* is to ask God for specific graces that we need in order to get closer to God and to realize our end, the purpose for which we have been created. The graces asked for may be an interior disposition like a desire for some spiritual gift or to make amends for sin, an outward emotion like joy, sadness, or grief, or even some more concrete experience like poverty or persecution in solidarity with Jesus.

☐ The Annunciation[1]

St. Luke writes in the first Chapter [26–39].

First Point. The first Point is that the Angel St. Gabriel, saluting Our Lady, announced to her the Conception of Christ our Lord. "The Angel entering where Mary was, saluted her saying: 'Hail full of grace. Thou shalt conceive in thy womb and shalt bring forth a son.'"

Second Point. The second, the Angel confirms what he said to Our Lady, telling of the conception of St. John Baptist, saying to her: "'And behold thy cousin Elizabeth hath conceived a son in her old age.'"

Third Point. The third, Our Lady answered the Angel: "'Behold the handmaid of the Lord: be it done to me according to thy word!'"

THE SPIRITUAL EXERCISES

Composing the Place and Hearing the Call

First Prelude. The first Prelude is a composition,[2] seeing the place: it will be here to see with the sight of the imagination, the synagogues, villages and towns through which Christ our Lord preached.

Second Prelude. The second, to ask for the grace[3] which I want: it will be here to ask grace of our Lord that I may not be deaf to His call, but ready and diligent to fulfill His most Holy Will.

THE SPIRITUAL EXERCISES

1 Ignatius is most thorough in outlining the steps for these two contemplations for the "second week" of the exercises. In a later appendix, he offers suggestions of various contemplations, referencing a particular scripture passage, and offering only brief instructions, assuming that having the example of the first two contemplations, we will be able to pray through other scriptural stories in the same way. In the case of this meditation, he suggests using Luke 2:1–7:

> In those days a decree went out from Emperor Augustus that all the world should be registered. This was the first registration and was taken while Quirinius was governor of Syria. All went to their own towns to be registered. Joseph also went from the town of Nazareth in Galilee to Judea, to the city of David called Bethlehem, because he was descended from the house and family of David. He went to be registered with Mary, to whom he was engaged and who was expecting a child. While they were there, the time came for her to deliver her child. And she gave birth to her firstborn son and wrapped him in bands of cloth, and laid him in a manger, because there was no place for them in the inn.

2 One of the key components of Ignatian contemplation is, as he suggests here, finding "myself present" in the scene which is unfolding. Yet, those making the Ignatian exercises often struggle with precisely how to do so. This particular contemplation is helpful for understanding this, as Ignatius gives fairly explicit instructions as to how we might imagine ourselves into the scene of Jesus's birth in the stable.

☐ Contemplation on the Nativity[1]

First Prelude. The first Prelude is the narrative and it will be here how Our Lady went forth from Nazareth, about nine months with child, as can be piously meditated, seated on an ass, and accompanied by Joseph and a maid, taking an ox, to go to Bethlehem to pay the tribute which Caesar imposed on all those lands.

Second Prelude. The second, a composition, seeing the place. It will be here to see with the sight of the imagination the road from Nazareth to Bethlehem; considering the length and the breadth, and whether such road is level or through valleys or over hills; likewise looking at the place or cave of the Nativity, how large, how small, how low, how high, and how it was prepared.

First Point. The first Point is to see the persons; that is, to see Our Lady and Joseph and the maid, and, after His Birth, the Child Jesus, I making myself a poor creature and a wretch of an unworthy slave, looking at them and serving them in their needs, with all possible respect and reverence, as if I found myself present; and then to reflect on myself in order to draw some profit.[2]

Second Point. The second, to look, mark and contemplate what they are saying, and, reflecting on myself, to draw some profit.

Third Point. The third, to look and consider what they are doing, as going a journey and laboring, that the Lord may be born in the greatest poverty; and as a termination of so many labors—of hunger, of thirst, of heat and of cold, of injuries and affronts—that He may die on the Cross; and all this for me: then reflecting, to draw some spiritual profit.

THE SPIRITUAL EXERCISES

1 During the third week, the retreatant is to meditate on Jesus's final days on earth, including his journey to Jerusalem, final supper with his disciples, arrest, and crucifixion. We see his suffering and the gift of the Eucharist as the ultimate expression of God's love.

□ The Third Week[1]

First Prelude. The first Prelude is to bring to memory the narrative; which is here how Christ our Lord sent two Disciples from Bethany to Jerusalem to prepare the Supper, and then He Himself went there with the other Disciples; and how, after having eaten the Paschal Lamb, and having supped, He washed their feet and gave His most Holy Body and Precious Blood to His Disciples, and made them a discourse, after Judas went to sell his Lord.

Second Prelude. The second, a composition, seeing the place. It will be here to consider the road from Bethany to Jerusalem, whether broad, whether narrow, whether level, etc.; likewise the place of the Supper, whether large, whether small, whether of one kind or whether of another.

Third Prelude. The third, to ask for what I want. It will be here grief, feeling and confusion because for my sins the Lord is going to the Passion.

The Spiritual Exercises

1 Here we are called to imagine ourselves as one of the disciples eating with Jesus at his last supper. Here and elsewhere Ignatius is encouraging us to use the full range of our senses and to see that our encounters with God can take place at various times, often outside the deliberate time we set aside for prayer.

2 The imaginative encounter with Jesus that we have in our contemplation of scripture can also be entered into in our everyday actions when we, as Ignatius suggests, imagine ourselves doing them with Jesus. In this way, we can see to imitating Jesus not only in the more radical aspects of his life but also in his ordinary manner and activities.

3 The advantage of this type of prayer is that we become more fully engaged in it, bringing our physical body into concert with our mind and imagination. The everyday movements of our body also become a way of imitating Jesus.

4 The movement of the exercises is to so draw together our experience and imagination that we might experience Jesus's crucifixion and death as if it were happening right now, before us, and to react accordingly.

5 Here Ignatius encourages us to use our imagination to enter into Jesus's experience in order to feel greater solidarity with Jesus and compassion for his suffering, and the suffering of others.

6 This is one of Ignatius's most interesting insights. It was very important to him that the one praying the exercises be able to imagine Jesus entering fully into human experience. Thus he suggests understanding the relationship of Jesus's humanity and divinity in a very specific way—insofar as Jesus was divine, he was capable of "hiding" that divinity from himself, allowing him to experience his life, suffering, and death in a fully human way. Ignatius is not pretending to know the dogmatic truth about Jesus's divine and human nature but just suggesting a way of understanding it conducive to the goal of the exercises.

☐ Imagining Jesus

While the person is eating,[1] let him consider as if he saw Christ our Lord eating with His Apostles, and how He drinks and how He looks and how He speaks; and let him see to imitating Him.[2] So that the principal part of the intellect shall occupy itself in the consideration of Christ our Lord, and the lesser part in the support of the body; because in this way he will get greater system and order as to how he ought to behave and manage himself.[3]

THE SPIRITUAL EXERCISES

Grace of the Third Week

It belongs to the Passion to ask for grief with Christ in grief, anguish with Christ in anguish, tears and interior pain at such great pain which Christ suffered for me.[4]

THE SPIRITUAL EXERCISES

Points for the Third Week

Fourth Point. The fourth, to consider that which Christ our Lord is suffering in His Humanity, or wants to suffer, according to the passage which is being contemplated, and here to commence with much vehemence and to force myself to grieve, be sad and weep, and so to labor through the other points which follow.[5]

Fifth Point. The fifth, to consider how the Divinity hides Itself, that is, how It could destroy Its enemies and does not do it, and how It leaves the most sacred Humanity to suffer so very cruelly.[6]

Sixth Point. The sixth, to consider how He suffers all this for my sins, etc.; and what I ought to do and suffer for Him.

THE SPIRITUAL EXERCISES

45

1 The fourth and last week begins with a group of meditations on the events that took place after Jesus's death on the cross, both those taken from Christian tradition, like Jesus's descent into hell, and those recorded in scripture, such as his appearances to the women at the tomb and to the apostles. The final week invites us to reflect upon the mystery of Jesus's resurrection from the dead, the love he has for his friends and for us, and the ways in which Jesus continues to live with us and labor for us in our everyday lives.

2 Here Ignatius asks us to visualize the "Holy Sepulchre," in this case referring to the tomb in which Jesus was buried. In Jerusalem one can visit the church of the Holy Sepulchre, a sacred site for many Christians thought not only to mark the location of Jesus's tomb, but also the hill of Golgotha, where Jesus was crucified.

3 The belief that the first person that Jesus appeared to after the resurrection was his mother, Mary, is a devotional belief that has been held by many Christians, including Ignatius, over the centuries. However, since there is no account of this in scripture, this, as with the meditation on the undocumented youth of Jesus, is a meditation which requires greater use of the imagination. Since some devotional beliefs with regard to Mary are not universally held among Christians, some may also choose to omit this meditation.

4 Ignatius goes on to describe how, after his appearance to his mother, Mary, the risen Jesus also appeared thirteen more times to his followers, both women and men. In this first contemplation, Jesus appears to his mother to assure her that he is not dead but alive. This series of meditations ends with Jesus's ascension into heaven.

☐ The Fourth Week[1]

First Prelude. The first Prelude is the narrative, which is here how, after Christ expired on the Cross, and the Body, always united with the Divinity, remained separated from the Soul, the blessed Soul, likewise united with the Divinity, went down to Hell, and taking from there the just souls, and coming to the Sepulchre[2] and being risen, He appeared to His Blessed Mother in Body and in Soul.[3]

Second Prelude. The second, a composition, seeing the place; which will be here to see the arrangement of the Holy Sepulchre and the place or house of Our Lady, looking at its parts in particular; likewise the room, the oratory, etc.

Third Prelude. The third, to ask for what I want, and it will be here to ask for grace to rejoice and be glad intensely at so great glory and joy of Christ our Lord.

First Point, Second Point, and Third Point. Let the first, second and third Points be the same usual ones which we took in the Supper of Christ our Lord.

Fourth Point. The fourth, to consider how the Divinity, which seemed to hide Itself in the Passion, now appears and shows Itself so marvelously in the most holy Resurrection by Its true and most holy effects.[4]

THE SPIRITUAL EXERCISES

1 Repeatedly throughout the exercises, Ignatius juxtaposes this sense of gratitude for great overarching gifts like creation and redemption with gratitude for the particular gifts given to each one of us.

2 This is the prayer that we are encouraged to pray at the end of the exercises. Even if we cannot live up to the demands of this prayer, Ignatius hopes that having completed the exercises, we can nevertheless do so with sincerity of heart and intention, thus blessing both God and ourselves. This prayer is one of the most dear to Jesuits. The act of giving over of one's self completely, though only occasionally realized and difficult to maintain, is at the very heart of a Jesuit's identity and desires.

☐ Gratitude

First Point. The First Point is, to bring to memory the benefits received, of Creation, Redemption and particular gifts, pondering with much feeling how much God our Lord has done for me, and how much He has given me of what He has, and then the same Lord desires to give me Himself as much as He can, according to His Divine ordination.[1]

And with this to reflect on myself, considering with much reason and justice, what I ought on my side to offer and give to His Divine Majesty, that is to say, everything that is mine, and myself with it, as one who makes an offering with much feeling:

Take, Lord, and receive all my liberty, my memory, my intellect, and all my will—all that I have and possess. Thou gavest it to me: to Thee, Lord, I return it! All is Thine, dispose of it according to all Thy will. Give me Thy love and grace, for this is enough for me.[2]

THE SPIRITUAL EXERCISES

1 This conclusion of Ignatius's spiritual exercises is called "The Contemplation to Attain Divine Love," and its goal is to further deepen the idea of finding God in all things. The meditation urges us to bring to consciousness the ways in which God labors for us in creation, and to be aware of how we, and all that lives around us in nature, are sustained in existence by the deliberate effort of God. This contemplation precedes the "Take Lord, and Receive . . ." prayer at the end of the exercises.

2 Though Saint Francis is more commonly associated with celebrating nature and creation, Ignatius also emphasizes the way God can be discovered and understood there.

3 Typical of Ignatian prayer, and similar to some of Jesus's sayings in the gospels, this passage invites us to move from a broader and more universal experience of God's presence to applying the insights we find there to our own personal life.

4 This is also typical of Ignatius's approach in *The Spiritual Exercises*, as well is in the Constitutions of the Society of Jesus (the rules governing the Society of Jesus). He makes recommendations on how to proceed while leaving the option open to choose an alternative that might better facilitate our encounter with God.

5 Here Ignatius gives us another way to understand the presence of God—in terms of God's labor to maintain all of creation. This is similar to Thomas Aquinas's insight that all things *are* because God wills them to be. To think of God as a worker and laborer is also useful for reflecting on our own work and labor.

☐ Contemplation to Gain Love[1]

First Point. The First Point is, to bring to memory the benefits received, of Creation, Redemption and particular gifts, pondering with much feeling how much God our Lord has done for me, and how much He has given me of what He has....

Second Point. The second, to look how God dwells in creatures, in the elements, giving them being, in the plants vegetating, in the animals feeling in them, in men giving them to understand:[2] and so in me, giving me being, animating me, giving me sensation and making me to understand;[3] likewise making a temple of me, being created to the likeness and image of His Divine Majesty; reflecting as much on myself in the way which is said in the first Point, or in another which I feel to be better.[4] In the same manner will be done on each Point which follows.

Third Point. The third, to consider how God works and labors for me in all things created on the face of the earth—that is, behaves like one who labors—as in the heavens, elements, plants, fruits, cattle, etc., giving them being, preserving them, giving them vegetation and sensation, etc.[5] Then to reflect on myself.

Fourth Point. The fourth, to look how all the good things and gifts descend from above, as my poor power from the supreme and infinite power from above; and so justice, goodness, pity, mercy, etc.; as from the sun descend the rays, from the fountain the waters, etc. Then to finish reflecting on myself, as has been said.

THE SPIRITUAL EXERCISES

51

Part 3
Ignatian Prayer

~ *The Spiritual Exercises* are really the closest thing that Ignatius has to a prayer manual and, as we have seen, the exercises can be at times quite specific about what to pray for, but also often very general and flexible in the forms and structures of prayer that it encourages. When he is speaking to others about prayer, often it is in more of a remedial rather than prescriptive way, more indirect rather than direct. The following passage, one of the more extensive treatments of prayer in his letters, offers a good example of this. As insightful as this letter is, we can see that his primary intention in this case is to demonstrate that the approach to prayer he is discussing is wrong, rather than to teach the right way of praying. Nevertheless, in doing so Ignatius teaches us a lot about how he understands prayer.

1 In 1549 two Jesuits in Gandia, where the recipient of this letter, Francis Borgia, was Duke (and secretly a Jesuit since 1546), Andrés de Oviedo and Francisco Onfroy came to the conviction that engaging in lengthy hours of prayer each day was essential to the spiritual life. Oviedo, for his part, sought permission to undertake such a life in the desert for seven years. Onfroy, however, went much further, calling for reform in the church and the Society of Jesus along these lines. Learning of the two Jesuits' ideas and intentions, Ignatius wrote a lengthy assessment of them and their teaching in this letter to Francis Borgia. He begins his letter by acknowledging the possibility that new prophecies or revelations might be legitimate, but require careful examination, and then describes his own process of discernment, noting, "It is very useful and extremely necessary to examine such spirits." He concludes that Onfroy's proposals are not legitimate, and his letter is largely dedicated to explaining why he believes this to be the case.

2 The whole of chapter 17 of John's gospel is Jesus's prayer for the disciples at the Last Supper.

3 Jesus prays three times in the garden of Gethsemane that God let the "cup" of his suffering pass from him, but also that God's will be done (Mark 14:32–42; Matthew 26:36–46).

☐ What Does Prayer Require?

To say that a meditation of one to two hours is no prayer and that more hours are required is bad doctrine and opposed to the opinion and practice of the saints.[1] First, consider the example of Christ: although he sometimes spent the night in prayer, at other times he did not spend so much, as in his prayer at the supper[2] or his three prayers in the garden.[3]

(continued on page 57)

4 Jesus's agony in the garden is the first of what has been traditionally known as the "sorrowful" mysteries, which also include the scourging of Jesus, the crowning with thorns, the carrying of the cross, and the crucifixion.

5 The "Lord's Prayer," or "Our Father."

6 John Cassian, who lived in the fourth and fifth centuries, was a monk of the early monastic period. He collected the wisdom and rules of the early "desert fathers," monks who made their home in the desert, who are considered the founders of monasticism. This collection, known as the *Institutes*, is what Ignatius is referring to.

7 These definitions are taken from *Concerning the Orthodox Faith*, considered the most important work by the theologian and monk Saint John of Damascus, who lived in the seventh and eighth centuries.

8 Ejaculatory prayer is a short prayer meant to be memorized and repeated throughout the day, such as the "Jesus Prayer," in order to "pray without ceasing." Ignatius would have known that when Augustine speaks of ejaculatory prayer he, like Onfroy, speaks of praying at length but punctuating that prayer with the occasional repetition of certain words or sentiments. However, he also knew that Augustine, like himself, would insist that such prayer should not cause us to neglect our other duties.

9 Francis Borgia joined the Jesuits in 1546, after his wife's death, but did so at first in secret so as to be able to get his considerable affairs in order (including the care of his children). As the Duke of Gandia and member of one of Europe's most prominent families, the transition from nobleman to Jesuit, he knew, would not be smooth or easy. In 1565, he succeeded Ignatius as the third superior general of the Society of Jesus.

He is not going to deny that these were prayers, and nor will he claim that they exceeded one or two hours. They probably did not exceed an hour, considering how much of the night needed to be left over for the other mysteries,[4] etc. Second, this can be seen from the prayer Christ himself taught us:[5] he called it a prayer even though it is short and does not take more than one or two hours to say; one should not deny that this is prayer. Third, these can be seen from the example of the holy desert fathers, who regularly practiced prayers that did not reach an hour in length, as Cassian[6] tells us; they would recite as many psalms at a time, etc., as is done in the public services and offices of the Church—unless he maintains that these are not prayer either. Fourth, the same is seen today in the practice of the faithful, and even of devout persons, of whom not all but only a minority—in fact, very few—exceed two hours of prayer at a time. Fifth, if prayer is 'asking God for what is proper' and, to give it a more general definition, 'the elevation of the mind to God with pious and humble affection,'[7] and if this can be done in less than two hours and even in less than a half hour, how can he claim to deny the name or reality of prayer to anything that does not exceed one and two hours? Sixth, the ejaculatory prayers so much praised by Augustine and the saints would not constitute prayers.[8] Seventh, the students who study for God's service and the common good of the Church—how much more time than this does he think they should give to prayer if they are to keep their mental faculties in condition for the work of learning and preserve their health?"

LETTER TO FRANCIS BORGIA[9]

~ The question of how to pray and for how long is always contingent, according to Ignatius's approach in the *Exercises*, upon what is happening between us and God. In general, Ignatius advises that if we have time we should err on the side of doing too much rather than not enough. Yet, especially when it comes to time spent in prayer, extra time above and beyond the expected would be measured in minutes, not in hours. Time spent merely in silence, or contemplating our surroundings, would be time he would consider equally important.

1 This statement more or less sums up what Ignatius would consider the ideal disposition to have when we pray. Though he is speaking specifically of the exercises, the statement is consistent with Ignatius's more general approach to conversation with God.

2 Though Ignatius allows a certain amount of flexibility with regard to length and ways of praying, he is also adamant that one must devote sufficient time to prayer in order to achieve the desired result. Thus the reverse logic here, which ascribes lack of spiritual movements to lack of discipline in prayer.

3 Ignatius knew that prayer would not always come easily, and believed that some obstacles to prayer could be the work of the evil spirit. In order to combat these difficulties, he advises that we pray longer than we had planned, especially when we are strongly tempted to cut our prayer short.

~ When it comes to prayer, Ignatius prefers quality over quantity. Thus, the person leading or undertaking the exercises should not see it as a series of mediations and contemplations, all of which must be gotten through. Instead, he suggests that we repeat those prayers that prove particularly fruitful, even if it becomes necessary to omit other suggested prayers.

☐ How, and for How Long?

Fifth Annotation. The fifth: It is very helpful to him who is receiving the Exercises to enter into them with great courage and generosity towards his Creator and Lord, offering Him all his will and liberty, that His Divine Majesty may make use of his person and of all he has according to His most Holy Will.[1]

Sixth Annotation. The sixth: When he who is giving the Exercises sees that no spiritual movements, such as consolations or desolations, come to the soul of him who is exercising himself, and that he is not moved by different spirits, he ought to inquire carefully of him about the Exercises, whether he does them at their appointed times, and how.[2] So too of the Additions, whether he observes them with diligence. Let him ask in detail about each of these things.

Twelfth Annotation. The twelfth: As he who is receiving the Exercises is to give an hour to each of the five Exercises or Contemplations which will be made every day, he who is giving the Exercises has to warn him carefully to always see that his soul remains content in the consciousness of having been a full hour in the Exercise, and rather more than less. For the enemy is not a little used to try and make one cut short the hour of such contemplation, meditation or prayer.[3]

THE SPIRITUAL EXERCISES

1 Ignatius's earliest experiences of directing the exercises often took place as he was traveling. Thus, many of those whom he guided would likely have done so at home or close to home, and many also during the course of going about the everyday business of their lives. In the nineteenth annotation, which precedes this one, he describes just such a way of making the exercises in one's daily life. However, this twentieth annotation describes what he would consider the more ideal circumstances for praying the exercises—finding some place quiet, away from home, and free of distractions to pray. Indeed, today this is what we commonly understand as the normative way to make a spiritual retreat. Ignatius didn't invent the concept of a retreat, but he advanced the understanding of it in such a significant way that when he was officially canonized a saint in 1622, he was also named the patron saint of retreats.

2 This is a basic principle of Ignatius's understanding of prayer, especially retreats: God rewards us when we separate ourselves from friends and daily cares to devote ourselves to God alone. This is a good reminder for those of us who doubt whether God might speak to us, or who are anxious about whether what is being communicated in our prayer is coming from God or ourselves. It is not uncommon for such questions to arise in our prayer, because we know of our capacity to deceive ourselves. Ignatius would certainly approve of exercising some discernment about what we believe God to be saying to us, but he would also encourage us to trust that God will reward our efforts by offering insights and graces to us during the time of prayer.

☐ Separating Oneself From Daily Cares

Twentieth Annotation. The twentieth: To him who is more disengaged, and who desires to get all the profit he can, let all the spiritual exercises be given in the order in which they follow. In these he will, ordinarily, more benefit himself, the more he separates himself from all friends and acquaintances and from all earthly care, as by changing from the house where he was dwelling, and taking another house or room to live in, in as much privacy as he can, so that it be in his power to go each day to Mass and to Vespers, without fear that his acquaintances will put obstacles in his way.[1]

From this isolation three chief benefits, among many others, follow. The first is that a man, by separating himself from many friends and acquaintances, and likewise from many not well-ordered affairs, to serve and praise God our Lord, merits no little in the sight of His Divine Majesty.

The second is, that being thus isolated, and not having his understanding divided on many things, but concentrating his care on one only, namely, on serving his Creator and benefiting his own soul, he uses with greater freedom his natural powers, in seeking with diligence what he so much desires.

The third: the more our soul finds itself alone and isolated, the more apt it makes itself to approach and to reach its Creator and Lord, and the more it so approaches Him, the more it disposes itself to receive graces and gifts from His Divine and Sovereign Goodness.[2]

THE SPIRITUAL EXERCISES

≈ Ignatius has heard that a former companion who had cheated him out of some money has fallen ill, and he decides to go visit him in hopes that he can offer him some spiritual consolation. As he prays over his decision, he is overcome with fear, though it is not completely clear why. He undoubtedly has some anxiety about his health, but he also may be fearful about how he will be received by this person, given the strain in their relationship. He perseveres in his journey despite the fears that continue to beset him. As he nears the end of his journey, and the fears are lifted, we see Ignatius engaging in a much more spontaneous form of prayer, shouting aloud with joy, and speaking to God openly and without hesitation. In this instance, Ignatius describes another form of prayer, one that cannot be carefully explained or outlined in the ways others are in the *Exercises*. For Ignatius, prayer can also mean simple surrender to consolation, and spontaneous expression of joy because of that consolation.

1 Ignatius offers a courageous example of what he considered to be one of the most important acts of charity we can extend to others. Clearly he felt wronged by the Spaniard, but although it may have contributed to his fear, Ignatius considered offering his presence and help to the man during his illness as more important than any grudge he might have against him.

2 By "tempting God" he seems to mean choosing not to travel fasting and on foot, thus foregoing the spiritual benefit for him and for his friend that he hoped would come from such a sacrifice.

3 Legend has it that the garment which Ignatius refers to was Jesus's seamless garment, which was taken from him prior to the crucifixion. The emperor Charlemagne, it is said, received the garment as a gift from his wife, and later gave it to his daughter who was abbess of the monastery in Argenteuil. However, earlier accounts suggest that the garment was instead one worn by the child Jesus, woven by his mother. In either case, Ignatius seems to be suggesting that his proximity to the holy relic had some role in relieving his fear.

☐ Spontaneous Prayer

The Spaniard with whom he had stayed at the beginning and who had spent his money without paying it back set out for Spain by way of Rouen; and awaiting passage at Rouen, he fell sick. While he was thus ill, the pilgrim learned this from a letter of his and felt the desire to visit and help him. He also thought that in those circumstances he could win him over to leave the world and give himself completely to the service of God.[1]

In order to achieve this he felt the desire to walk the twenty-eight leagues from Paris to Rouen barefoot, without eating or drinking. As he prayed over this, he felt very afraid. At last he went to St. Dominic's and there he decided to go in the manner just mentioned, the great fear he had of tempting God now passed.[2]

He got up early the next day, the morning that he was going to set out. As he began to dress, such a great fear came over him that he seemed almost unable to dress himself. In spite of that repugnance he left the house, and the city too, before it was quite daylight. Still the fear was with him constantly and persisted as far as Argenteuil, a walled town three leagues from Paris on the way to Rouen, where the garment of our Lord is said to be.[3] He passed the town with that spiritual distress, but as he came up to a rise, the thing began to go away. He felt great consolation and spiritual strength, with such joy that he began to shout through the fields and to speak to God.

MEMOIRS, 113–114

In this "second addition" Ignatius provides further insight into the use of imagination in prayer, giving specific examples of how we might imagine ourselves in some of the meditations and contemplations that make up the second week of the exercises. The images he offers might not resonate with us as they might have to a person of his time, but we can get enough of a sense of what he is suggesting to put our imagination to work and find images that speak better to our experience. So, we might imagine, instead of a king and his court, some other body that we might be ashamed to have failed—our family, our coworkers, our teachers, or our friends. The point is to imagine, by using images drawn from our own experience, what it would be like to stand before God with all our faults and failings exposed.

1 Ignatius frequently provides addenda through the course of the exercises, suggestions to improve or help along the experience. Thus the second week includes a series of "additions," the stated purpose of which is "to make the exercises better and to find better what one desires."

2 The midnight meditation helped to facilitate just the kind of process that Ignatius describes here. In essence, you are invited to ask God to wake you during the night for a time of prayer and, upon waking, immediately focus on the prayer at hand. Ignatius believed that prayer at this time, during an interruption in your night's sleep, allowed you to be especially open to the use of the imagination, and to the graces you could receive.

3 The examples which Ignatius offers here are not meant to imply that the contemplations should only be made with such a great awareness of our sinfulness and unworthiness. Rather, this is a reflection of the fact that this addition is to the second week of prayer immediately following the first, in which the main focus has been our sinfulness.

☐ Using Imagination in Prayer

Setting the Scene

Second Addition.[1] The second: When I wake up, not giving place to any other thought, to turn my attention immediately to what I am going to contemplate in the first Exercise, at midnight,[2] bringing myself to confusion for my so many sins, setting examples, as, for instance, if a knight found himself before his king and all his court, ashamed and confused at having much offended him, from whom he had first received many gifts and many favors: in the same way, in the second Exercise, making myself a great sinner and in chains; that is to say going to appear bound as in chains before the Supreme Eternal Judge; taking for an example how prisoners in chains and already deserving death, appear before their temporal judge.[3] And I will dress with these thoughts or with others, according to the subject matter.

THE SPIRITUAL EXERCISES

1 "Application of the senses" is another form of imaginative prayer that Ignatius frequently encourages. It is primarily a prayer of repetition, repeating a previous contemplation in a way that focuses on its sensual aspects. Throughout the exercises Ignatius encourages repetitions of various forms, especially when someone believes that he or she may have even more insights and graces to gain from what has already been a fruitful prayer period. The application of the senses makes this possible by engaging the imagination in a different way, one which may help one to experience a contemplation as more "real."

2 At this particular point in the exercises Ignatius is referring to the "first and second contemplation" on Jesus's incarnation and nativity. He does, however, suggest using the application of the senses for any contemplation and especially others he refers to explicitly later on.

3 The touching and kissing of sacred objects is a common Roman Catholic devotional practice. During mass, the priest shows reverence for the altar and the book of the gospels by kissing them. Similarly, Roman Catholics reverence the cross during the annual Good Friday service by processing to the front of the church to kiss or touch the cross. The application of the senses to prayer, therefore, is not as unusual as it seems, since many Catholics then and now would have had some experience of it in their devotional lives or experience of regular worship.

☐ Application of the Senses[1]

Prayer. After the Preparatory Prayer and the three Preludes, it is helpful to pass the five senses of the imagination through the first and second Contemplation,[2] in the following way:

First Point. The first Point is to see the persons with the sight of the imagination, meditating and contemplating in particular the details about them and drawing some profit from the sight.

Second Point. The second, to hear with the hearing what they are, or might be, talking about and, reflecting on oneself, to draw some profit from it.

Third Point. The third, to smell and to taste with the smell and the taste the infinite fragrance and sweetness of the Divinity, of the soul, and of its virtues, and of all, according to the person who is being contemplated; reflecting on oneself and drawing profit from it.

Fourth Point. The fourth, to touch with the touch, as for instance, to embrace and kiss the places where such persons put their feet and sit, always seeing to my drawing profit from it.[3]

THE SPIRITUAL EXERCISES

1 In this section of the second week Ignatius offers specific advice for contemplation and mental prayer, using texts like the Ten Commandments and the "Lord's Prayer," and learning to control the breath in order to enter more deeply into prayer.

2 The text of the Ten Commandments is found in Exodus 20:2–17 and Deuteronomy 5:6–21. This process of meditating on how one has failed with regard to these commandments is frequently suggested as a way that one might make an examination of conscience prior to confessing one's sins.

3 As in the Sacrament of Reconciliation, or confession, we are not invited simply to be aware of our sins or to confess them. Ignatius further emphasizes that we must also resolve to amend our lives.

4 In order to keep us focused as much as possible on prayer, Ignatius not only encourages prayer and meditation but also suggests that we measure our time in prayer in terms of prayer. Thus the "Our Father" and "Hail Mary" take on a dual role, as prayers that Ignatius encourages as part of many prayer periods, and as units of time. This also helps us to avoid the distraction of spending too much time on commandments that we know ourselves to have kept.

☐ First Method: On the Ten Commandments[1]

First let the equivalent of the second Addition of the "Second Week" be made; that is, before entering on the prayer, let the spirit rest a little, the person being seated or walking about, as may seem best to him, considering where he is going and to what. And this same addition will be made at the beginning of all Methods of Prayer.

Prayer. A Preparatory Prayer, as, for example, to ask grace of God our Lord that I may be able to know in what I have failed as to the Ten Commandments;[2] and likewise to beg grace and help to amend in future,[3] asking for perfect understanding of them, to keep them better and for the greater glory and praise of His Divine Majesty.

For the first Method of Prayer, it is well to consider and think on the First Commandment, how I have kept it and in what I have failed, keeping to the rule of spending the space of time one says the "Our Father" and the "Hail Mary" three times; and if in this time I find faults of mine, to ask pardon and forgiveness for them, and say an "Our Father". Let this same method be followed on each one of the Ten Commandments.[4]

(continued on page 71)

5 Ignatius means these methods to be pragmatic. The lists of commandments or deadly sins are not to be used to induce guilt or indulge in self-recrimination, but as a kind of checklist, so that we can realize which ones we are guilty of, and then focus on them.

6 In early Christianity, and even before, lists of more serious or "deadly" sins appeared in various sources, including texts of scripture and Greek philosophy. The seven sins now most commonly designated as the deadly sins—lust, gluttony, greed, sloth, wrath, envy, and pride—were compiled by Pope Gregory I in 590. They also appear in this order in Dante's *Divine Comedy*.

First Note. It is to be noted that when one comes to think on a Commandment on which he finds he has no habit of sinning, it is not necessary for him to delay so much time, but according as one finds in himself that he stumbles more or less on that Commandment so he ought to keep himself more or less on the consideration and examination of it.[5] And the same is to be observed on the Deadly Sins.[6]

Second Note. After having finished the discussion already mentioned on all the Commandments, accusing myself on them and asking grace and help to amend hereafter, I am to finish with a Colloquy to God our Lord, according to the subject matter.

THE SPIRITUAL EXERCISES

⟳ Many of us are accustomed to reciting the "Our Father," or "Lord's Prayer," in our regular worship, and often in our personal daily prayers. Though sometimes recited quickly without any discernible rhythm, this prayer is meant to be recited slowly, with a rhythm that is suggestive of the way in which this meditation might proceed. Those places where we tend to pause when reciting the prayer provide good stopping points for considering individual words or phrases that precede those pauses. The end of each line of the prayer, as presented below, for example, might represent the place we might pause to meditate:

> *Our Father,*
> *Who art in heaven,*
> *Hallowed be thy name.*
> *Thy kingdom come,*
> *Thy will be done*
> *On earth*
> *As it is in heaven.*
> *Give us this day*
> *Our daily bread,*
> *And forgive us our trespasses*
> *As we forgive those who trespass against us,*
> *And lead us not into temptation*
> *But deliver us from evil.*

1 Ignatius did not invent this type of prayer, which is a variation on the monastic practice of *"lectio divina"*—an early form of Christian prayer in which one chooses a particular selection from scripture or some other spiritual text to read through very slowly and meditate upon. What Ignatius proposes here is a sort of condensed form of *lectio divina*, in which the focus becomes even sharper. Someone might spend the whole hour, in fact, on just one of the lines of the prayer, or else meditate on the prayer in its entirety. It depends, of course, on how long one lingers in meditation on a given line. For example, meditating on

(continued on page 74)

☐ Second Method: Meditating on the "Our Father"

It is by contemplating the meaning of each word of the Prayer.

Addition. The same Addition which was in the First Method of Prayer will be in this second.

Prayer. The Preparatory Prayer will be made according to the person to whom the prayer is addressed.

The Second Method of Prayer is that the person, kneeling or seated, according to the greater disposition in which he finds himself and as more devotion accompanies him, keeping the eyes closed or fixed on one place, without going wandering with them, says "Father," and is on the consideration of this word as long as he finds meanings, comparisons, relish and consolation in considerations pertaining to such word.[1]

(continued on page 75)

"earth" might move us to consider the many variations of the word's meaning, whether it is Earth the planet, or earth as a synonym for soil, or we might be caught up in celebrating the beauty of creation, or be saddened by pollution and destruction of the environment. It might also suggest a connection with a specific past experience, a time perhaps when we nurtured the growth of a plant, fruit or vegetable. There are numerous possibilities for each word or phrase, as Ignatius suggests, and he also realizes that some words or phrases may stir little or nothing in us.

2 As we saw with the first two contemplations in the previous chapter on the annunciation and the nativity, this meditation is meant both as an invitation to meditate on the "Our Father" as well as a model for later prayers. Ignatius encourages us to do the same with any other prayer, especially those we believe might be especially fruitful. This might, for example, be an opportunity to enrich the experience of praying those "favorite" prayers we are especially drawn to but may not have focused on so intently.

3 This reflects what is more or less Ignatius's "rule of thumb" when it comes to prayer. While he is strict about the amount of time we give to prayer, even when our prayer seems dry and dull, or we lack motivation, he is not as concerned with "results." It is quite possible that we might spend an entire hour of prayer on only one or two "steps" in his outline, because we derived so much from them. This aspect of Ignatian prayer often proves hard for those who are accustomed to finishing everything they've started. So they might be inclined to abandon a particularly consoling or fruitful period of prayer out of fear that they might not "finish" it all, or they might feel pressure to extend the time of prayer considerably so as not to leave anything out. He warns against both these alternatives, inviting the person praying to trust that God can and does offer sufficient consolation and insight whether or not the prayer is completed, and within the time allotted.

And let him do in the same way on each word of the "Our Father," or of any other prayer which he wants to say in this way.[2]

Second Rule. The Second Rule is that, should the person who is contemplating the "Our Father" find in one word, or in two, matter so good to think over, and relish and consolation, let him not care to pass on, although the hour ends on what he finds.[3] The hour finished, he will say the rest of the "Our Father" in the usual way.

Second Note. The second note is that, the prayer finished, turning, in few words, to the person to whom he has prayed, let him ask for the virtues or graces of which he feels he has most need.

THE SPIRITUAL EXERCISES

⟩ These three methods of prayer begin to make apparent what we discover as we explore Ignatius's many different approaches. Ignatius seems to offer such a variety of suggestions for at least two reasons. First, we might discover which forms of prayer work best for each of us, and second, we can involve our whole person as completely as possible in the prayer experience. So, for example, he suggests a different measure of time for each form of prayer. In the first, the "Our Father" and "Hail Mary" serve as units of prayer time. In the second, one lingers on one portion of prayer so long as it's fruitful. In the third, each mini-meditation lasts only the length of a breath. He also is eager for us to get as much of ourselves involved in the prayer as possible, by means of the imagination, bodily by means of our breathing, and by involving our senses, as in the application of the senses.

1 Ignatius distinguishes between oral prayer and mental prayer. For the most part, Ignatius envisions prayer as mental, making use of our imagination, and reflecting on our experience. However, as we have seen, Ignatius generally suggests that a given period of prayer include the oral recitation of one or more rote prayers like the "Our Father" or "Hail Mary" and, in the case of the second method of prayer, for example, sometimes an equal portion of both.

2 This is a good example of Ignatius's desire to vary our prayer experiences. So, while he most often advises lingering on meditations or contemplations so long as they are fruitful, here he imposes a rather strict, short limit—the length of one breath. The intent here seems to be to invite us to consider those things which most immediately come to mind when considering each word that makes up a prayer, especially one we are already accustomed to praying frequently and orally, perhaps with little attention to the actual words of the prayer.

☐ Third Method: Rhythm

Third Method of Prayer. The Third Method of Prayer is that with each breath in or out, one has to pray mentally,[1] saying one word of the "Our Father," or of another prayer which is being recited: so that only one word be said between one breath and another,[2] and while the time from one breath to another lasts, let attention be given chiefly to the meaning

(continued on page 79)

3 Ignatius is not speaking of another person that might be sharing in the prayer, but rather the person to whom the prayer is addressed—God, Jesus, Mary, or one of the saints.

4 One of the results Ignatius hopes for from more focused reflection on these prayers is a greater sense of humility, especially as we consider ourselves in the light of God and his gifts.

5 The "Hail Mary" and "Hail, Holy Queen" are the most popular of the Roman Catholic prayers asking for Mary's intercession on behalf of the person praying, or their intention. "Soul of Christ," otherwise known as the *Anima Christi*, shown earlier in the text, was one of Ignatius's favorite prayers, so much so that its authorship is sometimes attributed to him.

of such word, or to the person to whom he recites it,[3] or to his own baseness, or to the difference from such great height to his own so great lowness.[4] And in the same form and rule he will proceed on the other words of the "Our Father;" and the other prayers, that is to say, the "Hail Mary," the "Soul of Christ," the "Creed," and the "Hail, Holy Queen," he will make as he is accustomed.[5]

First Rule. The First Rule is, on the other day, or at another hour, that he wants to pray, let him say the "Hail Mary" in rhythm, and the other prayers as he is accustomed; and so on, going through the others.

Second Rule. The second is that whoever wants to dwell more on the prayer by rhythm, can say all the above-mentioned prayers or part of them, keeping the same order of the breath by rhythm, as has been explained.

THE SPIRITUAL EXERCISES

1 What Ignatius refers to as "the examen" is in many ways similar to the traditional practice of the examination of conscience, by which we make ourselves aware of our sins, usually prior to confession. However, its purview includes more than just one's sins, because it is a method for recalling of the ways in which one has served and encountered God (or not) in the course of one's day. Jesuits are expected to engage in this practice twice daily. Over the centuries, many different kinds of people, whether lay or ordained, have found it helpful for their spiritual lives.

2 What we are expected to bring to this prayer is awareness of the many good things (including forgiveness for our sins) that we have received from God. In addition, the general attitude or feeling with which we should enter into our self-examination is one of gratitude.

3 We are meant to be grateful for the capacity to be aware of our sins, and the desire to live a life free of them.

4 As with the various methods of prayer Ignatius has advised, the examen too can be approached in various different ways, whether it be an inventory of certain types of sins that one is prone to—such as greed, envy, or self-deception—or by a more in-depth examination of one's experiences, feelings, temptations, and gifts received each hour of the day.

5 The last two points correspond to the requirements for a good confession. Having become aware of our sins, we confess them (in the Roman Catholic faith, this would involve sacramental confession to a priest) and, with the intention to rid our lives of these sins, we ask forgiveness from God for having failed in these ways. The fifth point, in fact, is expressed in words that one would use when speaking of the sacrament of penance. In order to receive forgiveness, one must have a "purpose of amendment," that is, the firm intention not to commit that sin again. We can also understand this in terms of our own attempts at reconciliation with others: we might be offended if someone were to offer us forgiveness for doing something for which we were not sorry. Similarly, we might also be reluctant to forgive someone who asked forgiveness without admitting to having done anything wrong.

☐ A Method of Self-Examination

Method for Making the General Examen[1]

It contains in it five Points.

First Point. The first Point is to give thanks to God our Lord for the benefits received.[2]

Second Point. The second, to ask grace to know our sins and cast them out.[3]

Third Point. The third, to ask account of our soul from the hour that we rose up to the present Examen, hour by hour, or period by period: and first as to thoughts, and then as to words, and then as to acts, in the same order as was mentioned in the Particular Examen.[4]

Fourth Point. The fourth, to ask pardon of God our Lord for the faults.

Fifth Point. The fifth, to purpose amendment with His grace.[5]

THE SPIRITUAL EXERCISES

1 This is taken from the same letter with which we began this chapter. Thus, "he" refers to Francisco Onfroy, who was not only insisting that the spiritual life (and Jesuit life) required numerous hours of prayer, but that we also could (and should) maintain a continual experience of the presence of God in our lives.

2 While Ignatius would not dispute the contention that God can be or even is continually present, his dispute with Onfroy is about the human capacity to be aware of that presence. We might translate "our state as wayfarers" simply as the "human condition." We are humans, not angels, incapable of focusing our minds on just one thing, even God.

3 As he does when disputing Onfroy's claims about lengthy prayers, Ignatius points out that even the greatest of saints could not achieve such an awareness. Human life requires us to be occupied with any number of needs and desires in our daily lives. That is why Ignatius advises getting away from such things in order to pray better. Yet, even, having gotten away, Ignatius knows that it would be impossible to spend that entire time in prayer, or even simply being aware of the presence of God. Even when we are alone with God and away from home, our mind can and does wander to thoughts of the different concerns of our lives.

☐ The Inevitability of Distraction

Fourth, what he[1] says about the supernatural state and the continual presence of God seems fantastical and false, for we do not read this even of the great saints, although some servants of God have a more continuous memory and more frequent actual thought of God than others. Fifth, it seems impossible in the ordinary course of things even for highly spiritual and holy persons, because such a presence requires an actual and fixed—indeed unmovable—attention in the intellect, something incompatible with our state as wayfarers.[2] Even very devout servants of God complain about wanderings and instability of the mind, and we read that St. John occasionally relaxed his contemplations by lowering his attention to a bird he held in his hand, saying to a follower of his who was disedified that, just as the bow cannot remain always bent, so neither could the understanding, etc. It is true that sometimes, even many times, numerous servants of God have a great and vivid awareness, quite certain and stable, of his eternal truths; but for them to remain permanently in this state is impossible to believe.[3]

LETTER TO FRANCIS BORGIA

Part 4
Choices and
Life Decisions

~ After the period of prayer on Jesus's early life, and before beginning prayerful reflection on Jesus's life of public ministry in the second week of *The Spiritual Exercises,* Ignatius invites us to begin to make choices about our life and how we will live it. This requires a disposition born of the prayer that has preceded this—an awareness of our own sinfulness that has arisen from the prayers of the first week, such as the prayer on the Ten Commandments. It also involves looking to Jesus's example of obedience to his parents, and above all to God, which is modeled by the young Jesus in both the scriptural accounts of his early life and the prayers of contemplation we have made both on those passages and on the "hidden life" of Jesus. This is all to be done with an eye to making certain basic choices in the contemplations that follow: choosing to follow Jesus or Satan, "the enemy of human nature," and to consider the fundamental choices we might make about our life that might reflect upon or even indicate whom we have chosen to follow.

1 As can be seen by Jesus's conversation with the rich young man in Matthew 19:16–22, the keeping of the commandments is the most basic indication that we have chosen to live our life in obedience to God. As is also apparent in this biblical story, however, once we have encountered Jesus, more is demanded of us: "The young man said to him, 'I have kept all these; what do I still lack?' Jesus said to him, 'If you wish to be perfect, go, sell your possessions, and give the money to the poor, and you will have treasure in heaven; then come, follow me.'" That is why Ignatius refers to this observance of the commandments as merely the "first state."

2 It is not completely clear from this context what Ignatius means by "evangelical perfection." However, when he mentions it elsewhere, he is usually speaking about religious life and, more specifically, the religious vows of poverty, chastity, and obedience, which are also known as the "evangelical counsels." Here, Ignatius seems to be speaking a little bit more broadly, but he certainly is referring to adopting a more radical life of following Jesus, similar to Jesus's invitation to the rich young man.

☐ Choosing with and for Jesus

First Preamble. The example which Christ our Lord, being under obedience to His parents, has given us for the first state,—which consists in the observance of the Commandments[1]—having been now considered; and likewise for the second,—which is that of evangelical perfection,[2]—when He remained in the Temple, leaving His adoptive father and His natural Mother, to attend to the pure service of His eternal Father; we will begin, at the same time contemplating His life, to investigate and to ask in what life or state His Divine Majesty wants to be served by us.

And so, for some introduction of it, we will, in the first Exercise following, see the intention of Christ our Lord, and, on the contrary, that of the enemy of human nature, and how we ought to dispose ourselves in order to come to perfection in whatever state of life God our Lord would give us to choose.

THE SPIRITUAL EXERCISES

⟨∾⟩ This is one of the most developed of Ignatius's non-scriptural imaginative exercises. He unfolds a drama which appeals to all the senses to underscore the essential choice between good and evil. Here we are invited to imagine the ways in which both Jesus and Lucifer might appear and appeal to us in order to recruit us to their side. As a soldier and man of his time, he presents this choice using royal and military images, images which in our place and time might not necessarily prove an aid to prayer. We might then use our imaginations to frame the same fundamental choice in some modern guise, as a choice between two political leaders perhaps, or as a choice between two employers, or we might shape it in terms of an imaginative landscape taken from a favorite work of literature or film. Whatever form this contemplation should take, we should keep in mind its basic purpose, to reflect on the consequences of following whom we choose to follow, and our desires in that regard.

1 Images of "standards" and "commanders-in chief" indicate Ignatius's attraction to military images and metaphors. Though perhaps most apparent here, Ignatius also uses such images and analogies elsewhere, and the imagery proves difficult even for Jesuits today. Ignatius, given his rather flexible approach to prayer, would certainly have approved of the tack taken by many contemporary spiritual directors of encouraging those of us who do not find such images helpful to replace them with more familiar images that could communicate the same intention.

2 Ignatius does not pretend to be impartial about this choice. He wants it to be clear that only one of these choices, the choice to follow Jesus, can help us to reach our full human potential. As with Jesus's temptation in the desert, the devil might appeal to our baser desires, but Jesus shows us that true human freedom lies in dependence upon God. To choose to follow Lucifer rather than Jesus is, as the description "the enemy of human nature" suggests, to deny who we are meant to be.

☐ Choosing between Good and Evil

The Two Standards

The one of Christ, our Commander-in-chief and Lord;[1] the other of Lucifer, mortal enemy of our human nature.[2]

Prayer. The usual Preparatory Prayer.

First Prelude. The First Prelude is the narrative. It will be here how Christ calls and wants all under His standard; and Lucifer, on the contrary, under his.

Second Prelude. The second, a composition, seeing the place. It will be here to see a great field of all that region of Jerusalem, where the supreme Commander-in-chief of the good is Christ our Lord; another field in the region of Babylon, where the chief of the enemy is Lucifer.

(continued on page 91)

3 This prayer is not meant as much as an aid to making a choice as it is to aid awareness of the *consequences* of one's choices. Ignatius wants us, having imagined these battlefields, to see that only the knowledge and imitation of Jesus will lead us to authentic human life. Satan's intent is to deceive us and offer us things we crave with the sole purpose of drawing us away from the opportunity to become fully ourselves by following Jesus.

4 This description of the enemy's purposes provides very important insight into Ignatius's understanding of sin and vice. For Ignatius, what lies at the root of temptations to a life of evil and sin are the pursuit of honor, riches, and power. Again, as in Jesus's temptation in the desert, these are the promises that the devil makes in the hope of deceiving us.

5 Ignatius makes a clear distinction between this second point and the one that precedes it. While Satan sends out demons to spread his word and offer his temptations, Jesus sends not angels, but human beings. We are meant to understand Jesus's mission primarily as a human mission, one that depends primarily not on spiritual powers, but on the life and work of those people who choose to follow Jesus.

Third Prelude. The third, to ask for what I want: and it will be here to ask for knowledge of the deceits of the bad chief and help to guard myself against them, and for knowledge of the true life which the supreme and true Captain shows and grace to imitate Him.[3]

First Point. The first Point is to imagine as if the chief of all the enemy seated himself in that great field of Babylon, as in a great chair of fire and smoke, in shape horrible and terrifying.

Second Point. The second, to consider how he issues a summons to innumerable demons and how he scatters them, some to one city and others to another, and so through all the world, not omitting any provinces, places, states, nor any persons in particular.

Third Point. The third, to consider the discourse which he makes them, and how he tells them to cast out nets and chains; that they have first to tempt with a longing for riches—as he is accustomed to do in most cases—that men may more easily come to vain honor of the world, and then to vast pride. So that the first step shall be that of riches; the second, that of honor; the third, that of pride; and from these three steps he draws on to all the other vices.[4]

So, on the contrary, one has to imagine as to the supreme and true Captain, Who is Christ our Lord.

First Point. The first Point is to consider how Christ our Lord puts Himself in a great field of that region of Jerusalem, in lowly place, beautiful and attractive.

Second Point. The second, to consider how the Lord of all the world chooses so many persons—Apostles, Disciples, etc.,—and sends them through all the world spreading His sacred doctrine through all states and conditions of persons.[5]

(continued on page 93)

6   Ignatius's view of what leads to the virtuous life is more or less the opposite of whatever leads to sin and vice. We should embrace poverty and reject riches; we should be indifferent to honors, seeking not to be powerful, but to prefer humility. There are different levels of these virtues, depending on the life we choose. All should strive for spiritual poverty, but if we desire to follow and imitate Jesus more completely we should also pray for actual material poverty. If we would follow Jesus more closely, we should not just be indifferent to honors but also desire persecution and contempt in Jesus's name. Finally, those of us so called ought to forego even our own power of self-determination, placing ourselves fully at the service of God's will. It is clear from what Ignatius has written that while he believed indifference to riches, honor, and pride was the path to virtue, the radical desire to experience poverty, humility, and persecution was reserved for those who, like Jesuits, could make themselves more completely available.

7   From a contemporary point of view, to pray for suffering in this way might be considered masochistic. However, although this appreciation for the value of suffering is less pronounced in Christian belief today, it has always been part of the Christian way of viewing life in the world. Furthermore, a couple of things are worth noting about how Ignatius understands this. First of all, he encourages us to ask for things like persecution and poverty only insomuch as they help us to serve God. Second, it is clear that this is a gift given by God, not something actively sought out. In terms of Jesuit life overall, Ignatius would have seen experiencing such hardships as an indication that God's will was being accomplished. And, again, given Ignatius's emphasis on the imitation of Jesus, he would encourage us not to expect to live or be treated any better for preaching the gospel than Jesus himself was.

Third Point. The third, to consider the discourse which Christ our Lord makes to all His servants and friends whom He sends on this expedition, recommending them to want to help all, by bringing them first to the highest spiritual poverty, and—if His Divine Majesty would be served and would want to choose them—no less to actual poverty; the second is to be of contumely and contempt; because from these two things humility follows. So that there are to be three steps; the first, poverty against riches; the second, contumely or contempt against worldly honor; the third, humility against pride. And from these three steps let them induce to all the other virtues.[6]

First Colloquy. One Colloquy to Our Lady, that she may get me grace from Her Son and Lord that I may be received under His standard; and first in the highest spiritual poverty, and—if His Divine Majesty would be served and would want to choose and receive me—not less in actual poverty; second, in suffering contumely and injuries, to imitate Him more in them, if only I can suffer them without the sin of any person, or displeasure of His Divine Majesty; and with that a "Hail Mary."[7]

Second Colloquy. I will ask the same of the Son, that He may get it for me of the Father; and with that say the "Soul of Christ."

Third Colloquy. I will ask the same of the Father, that He may grant it to me; and say an "Our Father."

THE SPIRITUAL EXERCISES

1 One of the main purposes of *The Spiritual Exercises* and Ignatian spirituality in general is toward making an "election," which is the choice of what we would commonly call today as our "vocation" or "calling." Because Ignatius composed the exercises during the course of his own discernment about his future state of life, this discernment is central to what he understood his exercises to be about. Thus they are often understood to include an election by which we decide to dedicate ourselves to one kind of life rather than another—to marriage, to the single life, to ministry, and frequently in Ignatius's day, the call to the religious life under vows. Yet, this decision can also be about other matters, such as a course of study, a career change, or a move from one geographical area to another.

2 Ignatius's talk of "ends" and "means" here can prove confusing. This, in part, is due to the fact that the way things unfold in our lives is not always perfect. Sometimes we choose a way of living with only our immediate concerns in mind, and not our ultimate end. The purpose of the election is to try to make decisions about the course of your life in what Ignatius believes to be the proper order. As his exercises begin with the First Principle and Foundation, so should our decisions about our vocation in life. Thus, Ignatius might say, we should not choose to do something or set a direction for our lives simply because that is what we want to do, only to decide later how to conform that choice to God's will. Rather, we should place God's will for our lives (as expressed in his first principles) at the forefront, deciding how the ways we choose to live could achieve the end for which we are created. Ideally this period of discernment and reflection will take place before making serious and sometimes irreversible life decisions, like getting married or having children. But in cases where someone has already made such a choice, the election is more a matter of how to achieve your ultimate end in God within the limits imposed by the life you have already chosen (even if it was chosen for the wrong reasons).

☐ Choosing for Good

In every good election,[1] as far as depends on us, the eye of our intention ought to be simple, only looking at what we are created for, namely, the praise of God our Lord and the salvation of our soul. And so I ought to choose whatever I do, that it may help me for the end for which I am created, not ordering or bringing the end to the means, but the means to the end: as it happens that many choose first to marry—which is a means—and secondarily to serve God our Lord in the married life—which service of God is the end.[2] So, too, there are others

(continued on page 97)

3 It was common for clerics during Ignatius's time, and especially bishops, to receive special "benefices" (derived from the Latin *beneficium*, meaning "favor" or "support"), which were plum positions or material favors These could accompany their choice of a particular place to minister, or their elevation to the ecclesiastical hierarchy. From a contemporary perspective it might be seen as something like receiving a family inheritance, or receiving the extra benefits or bonuses that come with a job promotion, such as an expense account. Because this often caused priests and religious to focus much of their time on ambition and rewards rather than on the service of God, Ignatius was adamant that Jesuits should not become bishops.

It would not be an exaggeration to say that Ignatius had a much stronger sense of the permanence of life commitments than many of us have today. For Ignatius, if one chose to marry, or to commit oneself to priesthood or religious life, there was no going back on that commitment, even if it was done for the wrong reasons. Today, people often undertake such commitments with the understanding that if it doesn't "work out," they can choose to do something else—leave religious life, marry someone else, or choose to adopt a single lifestyle. Ignatius's insistence on the unchangeable nature of certain decisions, even if we can imagine exceptional cases where a commitment might be broken, can still help us to take the work of discerning God's will for our lives much more seriously. Choosing God's will for our lives is not a temporary thing but a promise to which we will ultimately dedicate our entire lives. This is in keeping with Ignatius's understanding that our life choices are meant to be a conforming of our will to God's will, and not God's will to ours.

who first want to have benefices,[3] and then to serve God in them. So that those do not go straight to God, but want God to come straight to their disordered tendencies, and consequently they make a means of the end, and an end of the means. So that what they had to take first, they take last; because first we have to set as our aim the wanting to serve God,—which is the end,—and secondarily, to take a benefice, or to marry, if it is more suitable to us,—which is the means for the end. So, nothing ought to move me to take such means or to deprive myself of them, except only the service and praise of God our Lord and the eternal salvation of my soul.

THE SPIRITUAL EXERCISES

Changeable and Unchangeable Elections

There are some things which fall under unchangeable election, such as are the priesthood, marriage, etc. There are others which fall under an election that can be changed, such as are to take benefices or leave them, to take temporal goods or rid oneself of them.

THE SPIRITUAL EXERCISES

| 4 | Ignatius's understanding of vocation, despite his insights into the perils of discernment, seems quite romantic. He believes that a divinely inspired vocation will be clear and untainted by personal ambitions or desires. However, he is not naive, noting that many of us err, mistaking our own selfish desires for a given choice of living for a true vocation. Some of us, he warns, will find ourselves having to discern God's will in a permanent vocation that we have chosen for ourselves, and not at God's prompting.

Lifelong Commitments

Third Point. Third: In the unchangeable Election which has already been once made—such as marriage, the priesthood, etc.—there is nothing more to choose, because one cannot release himself; only it is to be seen to that if one have not made his election duly and ordinately and without disordered tendencies, repenting let him see to living a good life in his election. It does not appear that this election is a Divine vocation, as being an election out of order and awry. Many err in this, setting up a perverse or bad election as a Divine vocation; for every Divine vocation is always pure and clear, without mixture of flesh, or of any other inordinate tendency.[4]

THE SPIRITUAL EXERCISES

1 Those who made the exercises after already committing to an unchangeable decision such as marriage, priesthood, or religious life could still complete the exercises, making an election of a less permanent kind, or none at all. While Ignatius seems to have envisioned this process of discernment largely in terms of major choices, he characteristically sees that this kind of prayerful consideration of a life choice could be applied to a variety of life decisions that did not require a lifetime commitment, such as pursuing a career or course of study.

2 This is an apt expression of the state of openness and purpose which Ignatius hopes would ground not only our experience of the exercises, but our entire spiritual life. The more we can cultivate such an attitude in our prayer and our daily lives, the freer we become to fulfill our purpose in God's design.

3 Ignatius recognizes that the second point is an ideal not easily achieved, and perhaps never achieved by most. Here he identifies for us what he takes to be two of the greatest obstacles to achieving our ideal—the intellect and the will. When making the exercises, we can hinder God's communication with us by "overthinking," such as when we fail to trust that God is speaking to us and then arrive at the conviction that what we are hearing in our prayer is just our own voice telling us what we want to hear. The will's power is also obvious when we find ourselves seeking not God's will so much as God's affirmation for doing what we've already decided. Ignatius's instruction to the Jesuits in the Constitutions of the Society of Jesus regarding obedience is apropos; he insists that a Jesuit must make the will of his superior (who stands in the place of God) his own.

☐ Methods for Making a Decision

First Point. The first Point is to put before me the thing on which I want to make election, such as an office or benefice, either to take or leave it; or any other thing whatever which falls under an election that can be changed.[1]

Second Point. Second: It is necessary to keep as aim the end for which I am created, which is to praise God our Lord and save my soul, and, this supposed, to find myself indifferent, without any inordinate propensity; so that I be not more inclined or disposed to take the thing proposed than to leave it, nor more to leave it than to take it, but find myself as in the middle of a balance, to follow what I feel to be more for the glory and praise of God our Lord and the salvation of my soul.[2]

Third Point. Third: To ask of God our Lord to be pleased to move my will and put in my soul what I ought to do regarding the thing proposed, so as to promote more His praise and glory; discussing well and faithfully with my intellect, and choosing agreeably to His most holy pleasure and will.[3]

(continued on page 103)

4   When we set about listing the advantages, benefits, disadvantages, and dangers of a given course of action, it is possible that fear of one or a few dangers, or the appeal of one or a few benefits, might overly influence our decision. This is why Ignatius emphasizes the need to give greater weight to the "inclination of reason" than the "inclination of sense," by which he seems to mean the sway of strong individual emotions or desires.

Fourth Point. Fourth: To consider, reckoning up, how many advantages and utilities follow for me from holding the proposed office or benefice for only the praise of God our Lord and the salvation of my soul, and, to consider likewise, on the contrary, the disadvantages and dangers which there are in having it. Doing the same in the second part, that is, looking at the advantages and utilities there are in not having it, and likewise, on the contrary, the disadvantages and dangers in not having the same.

Fifth Point. Fifth: After I have thus discussed and reckoned up on all sides about the thing proposed, to look where reason more inclines: and so, according to the greater inclination of reason, and not according to any inclination of sense, deliberation should be made on the thing proposed.[4]

Sixth Point. Sixth: such election, or deliberation, made, the person who has made it ought to go with much diligence to prayer before God our Lord and offer Him such election, that His Divine Majesty may be pleased to receive and confirm it, if it is to His greater service and praise.

THE SPIRITUAL EXERCISES

1 This method highlights what was for Ignatius one of the most fruitful approaches to prayer—the use of the imagination. Here, by imagining another person faced with the same decision in various circumstances, we are able to make a more objective decision about our own situation.

2 This is a method that would be helpful in guarding against the kind of emotionalism and subjectivity that is described above, and a means of being more objective. For in giving someone else advice about a decision, we are less inclined to be swayed by our own individual desires or fears. And, if considering them, we would be more likely to say something like, "If it were me ... ," thus providing ourselves with a better awareness of the inclinations which might get in our way. This, as with many other things Ignatius advises with regard to life decisions, not only affirms the importance of the imagination, but also demonstrates his keen insight into the workings of the human psyche.

3 Contemplation of our own death and final judgment are two things which Ignatius believes to be especially helpful in considering the decisions we make in the present. In Ignatius's view, if we live for God, then we do not live for the moment, but with our ultimate destiny in mind. Thus he urges us to consider which choice would be more edifying to others, and more clearly directed to the service of God. Furthermore, when Ignatius speaks of the "day of judgment," we can assume that he understands it as described by Jesus in the gospels—that day when those who have turned their backs on their obligations to God and to others are separated out from those who have been faithful. This conception of the day of judgment is also reflected elsewhere in *The Spiritual Exercises,* both when Ignatius gives instructions on almsgiving and when he inspires the fear of failing God in his contemplation on hell. By projecting our gaze so far forward, we can detach ourselves from the present and simultaneously consider what accounting we would wish to give that would not risk hell and separation from God.

☐ Another Method of Discernment

First Rule. The first is that that love which moves me and makes me choose such thing should descend from above, from the love of God, so that he who chooses feels first in himself that that love, more or less, which he has for the thing which he chooses, is only for his Creator and Lord.

Second Rule. The second, to set before me a man whom I have never seen nor known,[1] and desiring all his perfection, to consider what I would tell him to do and elect for the greater glory of God our Lord, and the greater perfection of his soul, and I, doing likewise, to keep the rule which I set for the other.[2]

Third Rule. The third, to consider, as if I were at the point of death, the form and measure which I would then want to have kept in the way of the present election, and regulating myself by that election, let me make my decision in everything.

Fourth Rule. The fourth, looking and considering how I shall find myself on the Day of Judgment,[3] to think how I would then want to have deliberated about the present matter, and to take now the rule which I would then wish to have kept, in order that I may then find myself in entire pleasure and joy.

THE SPIRITUAL EXERCISES

1 It is hard to determine precisely what amount of money "ten thousand ducats" would represent today. Suffice to say, Ignatius is imagining a scenario in which the persons in question have received a considerable amount of money. A helpful way of imagining this for us is to think of it as someone winning the lottery.

2 It is important to see that in each of these cases the primary intention and desire of the person is to remain disinterested ("indifferent"), and not to be weighed down by receiving such a great sum of money. In other words, each of the people whom Ignatius describes in this exercise has good intentions regarding the use of the money.

3 Unsurprisingly, Ignatius invites us to see each person's motive as primarily arising from the desire to serve and give glory to God as well as to save their own souls. Indeed, this is the attitude that Ignatius would desire for and perhaps even presume of anyone making the exercises properly. Nevertheless, as this exercise demonstrates, even those starting with this common intention can make any number of choices.

4 This first pair have the desire to be free of attachment to the money, but never do anything to achieve this detachment, and thus die without ever having achieved their desire.

5 The second pair determine to use the money for God's service, but do so by deciding for themselves how God's will might be achieved by doing so. Thus, while they achieve part of their goal of serving God with the money, they fail in never completely giving up their attachment or asking God *directly* how the money ought to be used.

☐ Choosing What Is Best

Prayer. The usual Preparatory Prayer.

First Prelude. The first Prelude is the narrative, which is of three pairs of men, and each one of them has acquired ten thousand ducats,[1] not solely or as they ought for God's love, and all want to save themselves and find in peace God our Lord, ridding themselves of the weight and hindrance to it which they have in the attachment for the thing acquired.[2]

Second Prelude. The second, a composition, seeing the place. It will be here to see myself, how I stand before God our Lord and all His Saints, to desire and know what is more pleasing to His Divine Goodness.

Third Prelude. The third, to ask for what I want. Here it will be to ask grace to choose what is more to the glory of His Divine Majesty and the salvation of my soul.[3]

First Pair. The first Pair would want to rid themselves of the attachment which they have to the thing acquired, in order to find in peace God our Lord, and be able to save themselves, and they do not place the means up to the hour of death.[4]

Second Pair. The second want to rid themselves of the attachment, but want so to rid themselves of it as to remain with the thing acquired, so that God should come where they want, and they do not decide to leave it in order to go to God, although it would be the best state for them.[5]

(continued on page 109)

6   For Ignatius, the third pair clearly embody the ideal approach to this situation. They become indifferent even to the point of disliking having the money, but their achievement includes remaining unmoved by that dislike. They put the money entirely at the disposal of God's will, whether that involves the sacrifice of giving all the money away, or the burden of keeping the money and using it as God asks them to. The money itself, and all the temptations or desires (for good or ill) that come with it, become fully secondary to God's will.

7   It is interesting that despite Ignatius's clear view that choosing poverty would be the more perfect life choice, the better choice in this meditation is not poverty but indifference to money. Surely this is because Ignatius was aware that only a few were called to actual poverty. Alternatively, this meditation seems to indicate his belief that most (if not all) people can achieve this state of holy detachment. The choices of the first two pairs in this meditation might be seen as the "easy way out"—either getting rid of the money and avoiding the temptation, or keeping it and using it without asking God how it should be put to use. It is obvious that Ignatius thought the more difficult option—being indifferent as to whether we keep the money or give it away, so as to freely respond to God's will for its use—was the superior and more perfect choice.

8   Nevertheless, Ignatius is quick to add that one should pray for a remedy if one finds in oneself a strong tendency to find poverty undesirable or even impossible.

Third Pair. The third want to rid themselves of the attachment, but want so to rid themselves of it that they have even no liking for it, to keep the thing acquired or not to keep it, but only want to want it or not want it according as God our Lord will put in their will and as will appear to them better for the service and praise of His Divine Majesty; and meanwhile they want to reckon that they quit it all in attachment, forcing themselves not to want that or any other thing, unless only the service of God our Lord move them:[6] so that the desire of being better able to serve God our Lord moves them to take the thing or leave it.[7]

Three Colloquies. I will make the same three colloquies which were made in the Contemplation preceding, on the Two Standards.

Note. It is to be noted that when we feel a tendency or repugnance against actual poverty, when we are not indifferent to poverty or riches, it is very helpful, in order to crush such disordered tendency, to ask in the Colloquies (although it be against the flesh) that the Lord should choose one to actual poverty, and that one wants, asks and begs it, if only it be the service and praise of His Divine Goodness.[8]

THE SPIRITUAL EXERCISES

1 Ignatius is trying to allay concerns that using human means to accomplish certain goals might imply a lack of faith. This is not a concern, especially in light of his founding principle, which endorses any means we might use (save for sinful means)—even human means—to achieve the end for which we are created.

2 Ignatius wrote this letter of reproof to Juan Alvarez after he accused the Jesuits of "bending the knee to Baal" because they had initiated legal proceedings against a Dominican who had attacked the order. Alvarez found the use of "human means" in this case to be improper and caused quite a stir in making his case known to several people in Rome. This is one of Ignatius's most stern and forceful letters.

3 Though he does not say so explicitly, this passage suggests that we might even find that what we think is a distraction is actually a way in which God is trying to communicate with us.

4 Many of us spend much of our day busy with jobs and everyday concerns that would seem to have little to do with God or ministry. Some of us just accept this as the way things are. However, when we are striving to live a life more deliberately concerned with God's purposes, this "temporal business" can be both distracting and frustrating. Ignatius offers us a different way of looking at this situation, suggesting that the extra effort required, and the frustration, can in fact be seen as evidence of a growing commitment to knowing God's presence in all aspects of our lives.

5 Manoel Godinho was a Jesuit who became the treasurer of the Jesuit college in Coimbra. He had related to Ignatius his struggles reconciling his work with the financial affairs of the college with his spiritual life and hoped to be relieved of his position.

☐ Choosing God's Service

In sum: the use of human means at the proper time, when directed purely to God's service, is not wrong, provided we keep our hope firmly anchored in God and in his grace.[1] However, with regard to not using such means when God dispenses from them by providing otherwise, or when there is no expectation that they will be of avail for his greater service, we are all in agreement.

LETTER TO JUAN ALVAREZ[2]

Although responsibility for temporal business may appear and be somewhat distracting, I have no doubt that your holy intention and your directing everything you do to God's glory makes it spiritual and highly pleasing to his infinite goodness. For when distractions are accepted for his greater service and in conformity with his divine will[3] as interpreted to you by obedience, they can be not only equivalent to the union and recollection of constant contemplation, but even more acceptable to him, since they proceed from a more vehement and stronger charity.[4]

LETTER TO MANOEL GODINHO[5]

1 When speaking of "times" when a choice to follow God's call might be made, Ignatius's first example is the kind of call that many of Jesus's disciples experienced. The presence of Jesus himself caused them to leave everything behind immediately and follow him. While few would deny this to be the ideal case, Ignatius most certainly knew that few would experience such clarity. Thus, he describes two other ways of experiencing God's call in which we might put our trust. The second is the type that we might expect to encounter when immersed in the experience of the spiritual exercises, as it requires a familiarity with the movement of various spirits, and a level of spiritual maturity that would allow us to discern between them. This type of calling, then, would be experienced only by those who are more advanced in the spiritual life, or who are engaged in the exercises. The third is treated at slightly greater length—and perhaps with a bit more emphasis—because it is the most common and, as a result, a more "ordinary" experience. Ignatius's attention to this more "quiet" calling also serves for us as a corrective to the expectations we sometimes have about our religious calling. Rarely do we experience extraordinary insight or mystical certainty when it comes to this aspect of our lives; for most of us, it is discovered in the quiet and ordinary experiences of our lives.

☐ Times for Making a Decision

First Time. The first time is, when God our Lord so moves and attracts the will, that without doubting, or being able to doubt, such devout soul follows what is shown it, as St. Paul and St. Matthew did in following Christ our Lord.

Second Time. The second, when enough light and knowledge is received by experience of consolations and desolations, and by the experience of the discernment of various spirits.

Third Time. The third time is quiet, when one considers, first, for what man is born—namely, to praise God our Lord and save his soul—and desiring this chooses as means a life or state within the limits of the Church, in order that he may be helped in the service of his Lord and the salvation of his soul. I said time of quiet, when the soul is not acted on by various spirits, and uses its natural powers freely and tranquilly.[1]

THE SPIRITUAL EXERCISES

2 Even in the case of a strong sense of calling, like that of Ignatius, we cannot always be certain of the exact details of God's will. For example, at first Ignatius thought God was calling him to become a missionary in the Holy Land. However, when that became practically impossible (since he was forced to leave Jerusalem by the church authorities), Ignatius found it necessary to discern things anew. This new path eventually led to the founding of the Jesuits. For this reason Ignatius always emphasized the importance of considering one's calling and mission in the light of practical realities. This way of approaching things is also evident in the early history of the Jesuits. The original conception of the mission of the Jesuit order, did not include or envision the founding of schools. Yet within the first decade of the order's existence, this became a distinctive Jesuit ministry.

3 Despite Ignatius's practical advice about being careful about those whom one might have reason to fear, such caution has its limits. The common human vocation is to work for the good of souls and, as Ignatius insists here, nothing else should take precedence over that. The early Jesuits, especially those in new missions around the world, risked disease, torture, and even murder in their attempts to evangelize the peoples of Asia and the "New World." The decision to be careful or to take risks should not be based on fear or lack of it but instead based upon whichever course of action would best serve the primary goal of helping souls.

4 There is a significant thread in the Jesuit way of proceeding that encourages us to adopt an approach to ministry somewhat along the lines of what St. Paul recommended in his letter to the church in Corinth—to be all things to all people. Jesuits had dealings with both the rich and the poor and had to adjust their approach to ministry accordingly. Jesuit missionaries especially had to find ways to be accepted in the often markedly different cultures in which they found themselves by doing such things as learning local languages, partaking in local customs, and adopting local dress.

When Circumstances Change

After the pilgrim realized that it was God's will that he does not stay in Jerusalem, he continually pondered within himself what he ought to do; and eventually he was rather inclined to study for some time so he would be able to help souls, and he decided to go to Barcelona.[2]

MEMOIRS, 7

Our Vocation Is Not Safety

If all we looked for in our vocation was to walk safely, having to place the good of souls second to keeping far from danger, we would have no business living and dealing with our neighbor.[3] But it is our vocation to have dealings with all people. Indeed, as St. Paul says of himself, we should make ourselves all things to all people in order to gain all for Christ [1 Corinthians 9:22].[4] If we proceed with pure and upright intention, not seeking our own interests but those of Jesus Christ [Philippians 2:21], he himself in his infinite goodness will protect us. Indeed, unless his mighty hand held our profession fast, no avoidance of such dangers would avail to keep us from falling into them and worse.

LETTER TO DIEGO MIRÓ

≈ Few statements sum up the Christian vocation as eloquently and briefly as this one. What is particularly striking is that it seems no less pertinent today than it was in Ignatius's day. Though we might use slightly different language to express it, any Christian today, especially those who feel especially called to a specific ministry or vocation, can take these words to heart and be inspired by them.

☐ A Deep Bond with Jesus

To sum up my meaning in a few words: If you thought carefully about how deeply you are bound to defend the honor of Jesus Christ and the salvation of your neighbor, you would see how much you are obliged to dispose yourselves for every toil and labor to make yourself apt instruments of God's grace for this purpose, particularly nowadays, when there are so few real laborers, so few persons who seek "not the things that are their own but the things that are Jesus Christ's" [Philippians 2:21]; you need to strive all the harder to make up for what others fail to do, since God is giving you such a special grace in this vocation and resolve.

LETTER TO THE FATHERS AND SCHOLASTICS AT COIMBRA

1 Among the best ways of knowing what God is calling us to, according to Ignatius, is to take time to reflect on the unique set of gifts that God has given each of us. While our gifts may not be the sole determiner of our vocation, they point us in specific directions by which we may, along with prayer and attention to various movements of the spirit, come to realize it.

2 One of the main points Ignatius is trying to make in this letter is that the ways in which we may attain spiritual benefit, and the ways in which God works with us, change throughout the course of our lives. So while once Ignatius was pleased with the mortifications of the flesh and fasting that Borgia practiced, and which were fruitful for a time, he now realizes that Borgia has reached the point at which these austere practices are now harmful. Similarly we are also challenged from time to time to try a number of new ways to receive the gifts of God that our former devotional practices once provided and to discover the new means by which God intends to dispense grace.

3 Part of the reason our means of receiving God's gifts changes is that we grow older and sometimes fall ill. When this happens, various types of bodily deprivation become untenable, as we discover that the priority is to stay healthy for the service of God. The lesson is that we must not become attached to methods that have worked in the past but are no longer fruitful. We have to discover new and perhaps unexpected ways by which to let God communicate with us and bless us with the gifts that we need to serve God well, body and soul.

Our Gifts Point the Way

However, while in themselves the third sort are more perfect than the second, and the second than the first, for any individual person the best is where God our Lord most communicates himself through a manifestation of his holy graces and spiritual gifts. For he sees and knows what is best for the person and, knowing all things, points out to him the way.[1] To discover his way, it is useful for us, with the help of his grace, to seek out and try a number of ways so as to tread the one made clearest to us, as the happiest and most blessed in this life and wholly directed and ordered to the other everlasting life—whereby we are encompassed and made one with these most holy gifts.[2] I refer to those that are not in our own power to summon up as we wish, but are sheer gifts of him who gives and can effect all that is good. Such are—with his Divine Majesty as their goal and scope—a deepening of faith, of hope, of charity; spiritual joy and repose, tears, intense consolation, elevation of mind, divine impressions and illuminations—along with all other spiritual tastes and perceptions which are ordered to these gifts, with humility and reverence towards our holy mother the Church and her established rulers and teachers. Any of these most holy gifts should be preferred to all bodily acts; the latter have value only so far as they contribute to obtaining these gifts, or a part of them ... Hence, when the body is jeopardized through excessive hardships, the soundest thing is to pursue these gifts through acts of the understanding and other moderate practices, so that not the soul alone will be healthy but, with a sound mind in a sound body, the whole will be more sound and more fitted for God's greater service.[3]

LETTER TO FRANCIS BORGIA

Part 5
The Interior Life

1 Just previous to this Ignatius described an exterior vision he had been having. For a period of several days, he saw something hovering in the air near him "which gave him great consolation because it was beautiful." Later, as his internal vision became more attuned, he realized that these visions, while consoling, were not from God, but a distraction and temptation.

2 Here Ignatius describes a common temptation that can prevent us from starting a new life—the fear that we will not be able to sustain our commitment over time. We are tempted not to even try for anxiety or fear of failure.

3 Ignatius's early and rudimentary insights into the interior life are revealed here. From this moment on, Ignatius became increasingly aware of his interior movements, and how they compared to those of others. This growing awareness would eventually inform his insights about the discernment of spirits.

☐ Becoming Aware

Until this time he had remained always in nearly the same interior state of very steady joy, without having any knowledge of interior things of the spirit. The days while that vision[1] lasted or somewhat before it began (for it lasted many days), a forceful thought came to trouble him by pointing out the hardships of his life, like a voice within his soul. "How will you be able to endure this life for the seventy years you have to live?" Sensing that it was from the enemy, he answered interiorly with great vehemence, "Wretch! Can you promise me an hour of life?"[2] So he overcame the temptation and remained at peace.

Memoirs, 32

But soon after the temptation noted above, he began to have great changes in his soul. Sometimes he felt so out of sorts that he found no relish in saying prayers nor in hearing Mass nor in any other devotion he might practice. At other times quite the opposite of this came over him so suddenly that he seemed to have thrown off sadness and desolation just as one snatches a cape from another's shoulders. Now he started getting perturbed by the changes that he had never experienced before, and he said to himself, "What new life is this that we are now beginning?"[3]

Memoirs, 33

4   The director of the spiritual exercises is advised to stay in the background as much as possible, not getting in the way of what should primarily be a direct encounter between the one making the retreat and God.

Second Annotation.... For, if the person who is making the Contemplation, takes the true groundwork of the narrative, and, discussing and considering for himself, finds something which makes the events a little clearer or brings them a little more home to him—whether this comes through his own reasoning, or because his intellect is enlightened by the Divine power—he will get more spiritual relish and fruit, than if he who is giving the Exercises had much explained and amplified the meaning of the events.[4] For it is not knowing much, but realizing and relishing things interiorly, that contents and satisfies the soul.

THE SPIRITUAL EXERCISES

⁓ When we become more interiorly aware, we also become more conscious of how sin works in our lives. This new consciousness of sin could lead us to despair. The Ignatian exercises are meant to inspire sorrow for our sins, but the purpose is to put this heightened awareness to use to become better persons. To do so, we must avoid two major temptations: denial of our own sinfulness and excessive sorrow and guilt that might lead to despair.

1 Ignatius explains to Francis Borgia what he sees as one of the challenges of our growth in holiness—we become more conscious of even our smallest sins. We also realize that we will never completely overcome them.

2 In Ignatius's view, true advancement in the spiritual life will never inspire pride, only the humility of being even more aware of the things, both apparent and hidden, that get in the way of our relationship with God.

Fill in this card and return it to us to be eligible for our
quarterly drawing for a $100 gift certificate for SkyLight Paths books.

We hope that you will enjoy this book and find it useful in enriching your life.

Book title: _____

Your comments: _____

How you learned of this book: _____

If purchased: Bookseller _____ City _____ State _____

Please send me a free SkyLight Paths Publishing catalog. I am interested in: (check all that apply)

1. ❑ Spirituality   4. ❑ Spiritual Texts   7. ❑ Prayer/Worship
2. ❑ Mysticism/Kabbalah   5. ❑ Religious Traditions (Which ones?)   8. ❑ Meditation
3. ❑ Philosophy/Theology   6. ❑ Children's Books   9. ❑ Interfaith Resources

Name (PRINT) _____

Street _____

City _____ State _____ Zip _____

E-MAIL (FOR SPECIAL OFFERS ONLY) _____

Please send a SkyLight Paths Publishing catalog to my friend:

Name (PRINT) _____

Street _____

City _____ State _____ Zip _____

SKYLIGHT PATHS® Publishing Tel: (802) 457-4000 • Fax: (802) 457-4004
Available at better booksellers. Visit us online at www.skylightpaths.com

☐ Awareness of Sin, Resistance, and Faults

In the Spiritual Exercises, sins and their malice are understood more intimately, than in the time when one was not so giving himself to interior things. Gaining now more knowledge of and sorrow for them, he will have greater profit and merit than he had before.

THE SPIRITUAL EXERCISES

For one thing of which I am convinced (remaining open to another opinion from persons of better understanding) is that there are few persons in this life—indeed there is not a single person—who are capable of fully determining or judging how much they themselves hinder and prevent what our Lord wishes to work in their souls. Indeed, I think the more practiced and experienced a person becomes in humility and charity, the more he will sense and become aware of even the slightest thoughts and other subtle matters which impede and hinder him, though these may appear to be of little or almost no significance, being in themselves tiny.[1]

Even so, a full awareness of our resistances and faults is not something we can have in this life: the prophet prays to be freed from the faults he does not know [Psalm 19:12], and St. Paul, confessing he is unaware of any, adds that he is not for that reason justified" [1 Corinthians 6:4]."[2]

LETTER TO FRANCIS BORGIA

1 According to Ignatius, the will can act independently, but even then it often falls under the influence of the good or bad spirit. For Ignatius, the ideal is to turn one's will over entirely to God, effectively overcoming the bad spirit.

2 In his writings Ignatius often refers to the good spirit, and the bad or evil spirit. Identifying these spirits is essential to the interior life, and especially what Ignatius calls "the discernment of spirits." It is likely that he would have understood such spirits as supernatural entities (like angels or demons) working in the service of God in the first case, and in the service of Satan in the other. We might find these concepts and the language with which Ignatius describes them difficult to accept in our day and age, but we needn't believe in demons to recognize that some movements of the soul incline us toward God's will and others do not. Whatever we call the source of such inclinations, it is hard to dispute the benefits of distinguishing between those desires and impulses that encourage us in our desire to love and serve God better, and those that stand in the way.

3 The "enemy of human nature" is a phrase that Ignatius often uses to describe the devil or the evil spirit. It implies a positive view of human nature—although Ignatius grants that human beings are inclined toward sin, he did not seem to believe that human nature was inherently corrupt or evil. In this he resembles Thomas Aquinas, who also believed that human beings were basically good. In the theological perspective of the Ignatian exercises, Jesus, being human himself, would be seen as the "friend" of human nature.

4 Ignatius outlines here an important mode of reflection. He wants us to recognize that a series of good thoughts can still lead to two very different ends. If the result is good, and proceeds from a series of good thoughts, then we can be assured of its divine origins. But if the thoughts seem good and yet the outcome is bad, we can use an examination of the series as a means of identifying where the evil spirit was able to turn things, hopefully enabling us to avoid a similar problem in the future.

☐ The Different Spirits at Work in Our Lives

I presuppose that there are three kinds of thoughts in me: that is, one my own, which springs from my mere liberty and will;[1] and two others, which come from without, one from the good spirit, and the other from the bad.

THE SPIRITUAL EXERCISES

Identifying Them

Fifth Rule. The fifth: We ought to note well the course of the thoughts, and if the beginning, middle and end is all good, inclined to all good, it is a sign of the good Angel; but if in the course of the thoughts which he brings it ends in something bad, of a distracting tendency, or less good than what the soul had previously proposed to do, or if it weakens it or disquiets or disturbs the soul, taking away its peace, tranquility and quiet, which it had before, it is a clear sign that it proceeds from the evil spirit, enemy of our profit and eternal salvation.[2]

Sixth Rule. The sixth: When the enemy of human nature[3] has been perceived and known by his serpent's tail and the bad end to which he leads on, it helps the person who was tempted by him, to look immediately at the course of the good thoughts which he brought him at their beginning, and how little by little he aimed at making him descend from the spiritual sweetness and joy in which he was, so far as to bring him to his depraved intention; in order that with this experience, known and noted, the person may be able to guard for the future against his usual deceits.[4]

THE SPIRITUAL EXERCISES

1 Spiritual consolation, the sense of being connected to God and at peace in God's presence, is so important in Ignatius's vision of the spiritual life that he believes it would be difficult, if not impossible, for us to advance in the spiritual life without it. Though he would certainly have allowed for "dark night" spiritual experiences, he would see these as being beneficial mainly to those already well advanced in the spiritual life, who would make up only a small portion of those engaging in the spiritual exercises.

2 When Ignatius speaks of interior movements, he is referring to the ways in which God makes use of our passions, desires, emotions, and will to draw us deeper into relationship, inspiring us to act upon these movements in the discerning of God's will for our lives.

3 This form of consolation corresponds to the grace that Ignatius encourages us to ask for in the third week of the spiritual exercises, which focuses on the passion of Jesus: "To ask for what I want. It will be here grief, feeling and confusion because for my sins the Lord is going to the Passion."

☐ Consolation and Desolation

Of Spiritual Consolation.[1] I call it consolation when some interior movement[2] in the soul is caused, through which the soul comes to be inflamed with love of its Creator and Lord; and when it can in consequence love no created thing on the face of the earth in itself, but in the Creator of them all.

Likewise, when it sheds tears that move to love of its Lord, whether out of sorrow for one's sins, or for the Passion of Christ our Lord, or because of other things directly connected with His service and praise.[3]

Finally, I call consolation every increase of hope, faith and charity, and all interior joy which calls and attracts to heavenly things and to the salvation of one's soul, quieting it and giving it peace in its Creator and Lord.

THE SPIRITUAL EXERCISES

1 The "third rule" simply refers to the definition of consolation given above. These definitions of consolation and desolation are included in a section of *The Spiritual Exercises* that outlines "rules" regarding different movements of the soul.

2 Ignatius shared the belief of Saint. Augustine and many theologians before him that we are made for God, and that the desire for God is innate in every human being. This is obvious in his founding principle—"Man is created to praise, reverence, and serve God our Lord, and by this means to save his soul"—and is also essential to the understanding of what he means by desolation. Desolation, at its root, is a feeling of being separated from God, which manifests itself in general feelings of loneliness, anxiety, and despair.

3 This is one of Ignatius's most important principles of discernment. He recognized the human inclination to make rash and unwise decisions in times of stress and challenge. Therefore, this is not just a good guiding principle for the one making the exercises but for all our decisions in daily life. It is not unlike the kind of advice we might give to someone we knew to be suffering from depression, or someone struggling with grief, to put off decisions about quitting a job, moving, or any other drastic life change until he or she has achieved some peace of mind.

☐ Spiritual Desolation

I call desolation all the contrary of the third rule,[1] such as darkness of soul, disturbance in it, movement to things low and earthly, the unquiet of different agitations and temptations, moving to want of confidence, without hope, without love, when one finds oneself all lazy, tepid, sad, and as if separated from his Creator and Lord.[2]

Because, as consolation is contrary to desolation, in the same way the thoughts which come from consolation are contrary to the thoughts which come from desolation.

Fifth Rule. The fifth: In time of desolation never to make a change;[3] but to be firm and constant in the resolutions and determination in which one was the day preceding such desolation, or in the determination in which he was in the preceding consolation. Because, as in consolation it is rather the good spirit who guides and counsels us, so in desolation it is the bad, with whose counsels we cannot take a course to decide rightly.

THE SPIRITUAL EXERCISES

1 It seems that all of us can feel desolate at those times when we feel as if we are doing all the work in our relationship with God—our prayers are not answered, Sunday worship is drudgery, and we can't seem to get anything out of spiritual practices that previously gave us joy, such as giving glory to God through our service to others or to the church. We begin to think that God isn't meeting us halfway by providing us with opportunities for joy, or with the graces that we need.

2 This list of its principal causes doesn't wholly account for what Ignatius describes as desolation. He gives the impression that desolation has two main causes, either our own willfulness and sin, or the action of God testing us in some way. Yet I think Ignatius would be ready to acknowledge, especially if he had the benefit of modern psychology, that there are times when the cause of desolation seem neither our fault nor God's. Many would hesitate today, for example, to say of someone who is suffering depression that it is their fault, or that God is testing them, although that is probably how Ignatius would have understood it.

Ignatius prefers to understand the "principal" causes of desolation in terms of the person's relationship with God. In this light, desolation is seen primarily as the result of our own sinful desires and actions, or as a challenge to persevere in our relationship with God or (and perhaps overall) as a way of reminding us of our need to trust in God and God's grace completely. This is not such a bad approach to understanding our own hardships—examining the ways in which we might be responsible for them, and reflecting upon what they might be challenging us to in terms of our relationship with God. This, while also acknowledging that there may be experiences of desolation (as in the case of clinical depression, for example) that we might be hard-pressed to attribute to our own actions, or God's action.

☐ Causes of Desolation

There are three principal reasons why we find ourselves desolate.

The first is, because of our being tepid, lazy, or negligent in our spiritual exercises; and so through our faults, spiritual consolation withdraws from us.

The second, to try us and see how much we are and how much we let ourselves out in His service and praise without such great pay of consolation and great graces.[1]

The third, to give us true acquaintance and knowledge, that we may interiorly feel that it is not ours to get or keep great devotion, intense love, tears, or any other spiritual consolation, but that all is the gift and grace of God our Lord, and that we may not build a nest in a thing not ours, raising our intellect into some pride or vainglory, attributing to us devotion or the other things of the spiritual consolation.[2]

THE SPIRITUAL EXERCISES

1 Since *The Spiritual Exercises* begins with a week of meditation on our own sin, it will come as no surprise that Ignatius encourages awareness of our personal faults. Indeed, Ignatian spirituality, as this letter suggests, never concedes an incapacity for change. In Ignatius's vision, the person aware of his or her own faults and failings can always become better and advance in holiness.

2 Ignatius is offering practical wisdom here—know what you are capable of and what you are not. This is also a warning against excessive pridefulness, the kind that leads to self-deception about what you can accomplish.

3 This is one of a series of instructions written by Ignatius to Stefano Baroello, who was a Jesuit priest being sent to Sicily to minister to children, assisting a priest of another order who worked with the Jesuits establishing orphanages.

☐ Self-Awareness

Regarding personal faults, it is certainly necessary that anyone with self-knowledge should acknowledge them in himself. In our present wretched state, no one can help having them, until all the evil that is in us has been utterly consumed in the forge of the eternal love of God our Creator and Lord, our souls being permeated and entirely possessed by him and our wills entirely conformed to—or rather transformed into—his will, which is rectitude itself and perfect goodness. But may his infinite mercy at least grant us all that we may every day regret and detest more deeply all our faults and imperfections; may he bring us to have a greater share in the eternal light of his wisdom and therewith to keep before us his infinite goodness and perfection, so that in its presence our smallest defects may become evident and unbearable to us, and we may attack and substantially weaken and diminish them with the help of God.[1]

LETTER TO TERESA REJADELL

Focus On Your Talents

Be universally careful to act with all humility in matters that are proportionate to your ability, and do not meddle with those that are beyond your powers; for God wishes to be served by each of us according to the talents he has bestowed upon us, and he is not pleased with presumption. Yet this should not in the least lessen your courage for vigorously undertaking whatever is within your grasp.[2]

LETTER TO STEFANO BAROELLO[3]

4 Here Ignatius addresses another dangerous form of self-deception: the belief that one can be free of bias. As he does elsewhere, he warns that those who are the most spiritually mature or prudent are, in many ways, those most imperiled by such arrogance.

5 This excerpt is taken from one of Ignatius's most famous letters, a series of instructions aimed at diffusing a dispute that had broken out in the province of Portugal over matters of obedience. The dispute was largely between the supporters and opponents of Simão Rodrigues, a co-founder of the Society with Ignatius, and the first provincial of the Portuguese province. These contentions came to the fore under the leadership of Rodrigues's more rigid successor, Diego Miró. Ignatius sent an official visitor who was unable to settle the crisis. By the time it had been resolved, about thirty men from that province had left the Jesuits. Since obedience was meant to be the hallmark of the Jesuits, this letter later became required reading for young Jesuits.

6 The origin of these spiritual counsels is uncertain, but they are thought to have been written and distributed among Jesuits a few years after the founding of the Society of Jesus in the 1540s. They are a series of suggestions for how to prudently go about one's ministry.

7 While Ignatius would find fault in someone whose moral life was motivated by excessive fear of God, he does acknowledge that, at least initially, it might be better than too little. In times like our own, when any kind of fear of God is often considered unhealthy, Ignatius's alternative suggestion is worth pondering.

8 Servile fear would primarily involve fear of being punished by God, whereas filial love would be more concerned with offending the God with whom one shares a deep love.

Guard Against Personal Bias

Thus, even in other human affairs wise persons commonly consider that it is true prudence to distrust one's own prudence—particularly in matters of personal interest, where, because of bias, people are usually not good judges.[4]

LETTER TO JESUITS IN PORTUGAL[5]

What If God Were Present?

We should not want to see or do anything which could not be done in the presence of God and of his creatures; and so we will always keep aware in our imagination of being present before him.

IGNATIUS'S "COUNSELS" [6]

Eighteenth Rule. Although serving God our Lord much out of pure love is to be esteemed above all; we ought to praise much the fear of His Divine Majesty, because not only filial fear is a thing pious and most holy, but even servile fear—when the man reaches nothing else better or more useful[7]—helps much to get out of mortal sin. And when he is out, he easily comes to filial fear, which is all acceptable and grateful to God our Lord: as being at one with the Divine Love.[8]

THE SPIRITUAL EXERCISES

1 Ignatius began to suspect God's activity in his interior life when his long-held desires for worldly glory began to dissipate while his new-found desire to be a saint proved more lasting. A frequent indication of advancement in the spiritual life is this experience of being motivated and even joyful at the prospect of doing something that we would have once sought to avoid.

2 Ignatius establishes these different "rules" based upon his observation that God works in us in different ways depending upon where we are starting from in our relationship. This is a most important insight related to Ignatius's realization above. What causes us pleasure or pain will be interpreted differently depending our state in life with regard to sin and our relationship with God. So, for example, excessive guilt would be the work of the good spirit for the thoughtlessly sinful person, whereas it would be the work of the evil spirit in those striving to live holy and virtuous lives.

☐ Interior Movements of the Soul

Yet there was a difference. When he was thinking of those things of the world, he took much delight in them, but afterwards, when he was tired and put them aside, he found himself dry and dissatisfied. But when he thought of going to Jerusalem barefoot, and of eating nothing but plain vegetables and practicing all the other rigors that he saw in the saints, not only was he consoled when he had these thoughts but even after putting them aside he remained satisfied and joyful.[1]

... Little by little he came to recognize the difference between the spirits that were stirring, one from the devil, the other from God.

MEMOIRS, 9

Different Movements of the Soul

First Rule. The first Rule: In the persons who go from mortal sin to mortal sin, the enemy is commonly used to propose to them apparent pleasures, making them imagine sensual delights and pleasures in order to hold them more and make them grow in their vices and sins. In these persons the good spirit uses the opposite method, pricking them and biting their consciences through the process of reason.

Second Rule. The second: In the persons who are going on intensely cleansing their sins and rising from good to better in the service of God our Lord, it is the method contrary to that in the first Rule, for then it is the way of the evil spirit to bite, sadden, and put obstacles, disquieting with false reasons, that one may not go on; and it is proper to the good to give courage and strength, consolations, tears, inspirations and quiet, easing, and putting away all obstacles, that one may go on in well doing.[2]

THE SPIRITUAL EXERCISES

1 As in similar insights, Ignatius is trying to point out that repression, like guilt, can take both positive and negative forms.

2 Ignatius seems to be arguing against the perception, still prevalent today, that repression is harmful or unhealthy. In the case of repressing sinful desires, Ignatius believes that it is often not only good, but the will of God.

3 This view of repression might seem a little surprising in light of the previous statement. His point is that while it may be spiritually beneficial to abstain from some non-sinful pleasure (such as giving up meat or desserts during Lent), we must determine whether such a sacrifice might be good for us personally, or whether it should be undertaken during times when our greater need is to strengthen ourselves, not make ourselves weaker.

4 While Ignatius emphasizes that we should always keep in mind God's will for our life, and the service of that will, he also knew the dangers of the kind of "workaholism" that he himself was prone to. This explains, for example, why he mandates that each Jesuit province have a "villa" to which the members can go for vacation and recreation away from work, separate from their annual retreat.

5 Casanova was a young teacher at the Jesuit school in Tivoli, who was seriously ill at this time. It is not known how well he followed Ignatius's advice, as Ignatius died eleven days after writing this letter, and Casanova himself died less than three years later.

☐ Repression of Desires

I received your letter, in which you assert that it is a certainty that it is the repressing of your sensuality which takes away your strength, and that you are therefore determined to concentrate on the main business of your soul.[1] First, although it could well be that this weakness of yours comes partly from such repression, I do not think it the whole cause; on the contrary, mental exercises, particularly immoderate and unseasonable ones, must also play a part ... Moreover, this repressing can be of two sorts. One is when through reason and light from God you become aware of a movement of sensuality or of the sensitive faculty which is against God's will and would be sinful, and you repress this out of the fear and love of God.[2] This is the right thing to do even if weakness or any other bodily ill ensues, since we may never commit any sin for this or any other consideration. But there is another kind of repressing one's sensuality, when you feel a desire for some recreation or anything else that is lawful and entirely without sin, but out of a desire for mortification or love of the cross you deny what you long for. This second sort of repression is not appropriate for everyone, nor at all times.[3] In fact, there are times when in order to sustain one's strength over the long haul in God's service, it is more meritorious to take some honest recreation for the senses than to repress them.[4] And so you can see that the first sort of repression is good for you, but not the second—even when you aim at proceeding by the way that is most perfect and pleasing to God.

LETTER TO STEFANO CASANOVA[5]

1 While Ignatius was clearly not averse to spiritual enlightenment and consolations, he learned to be much more strict and practical when it came to prayer, setting aside sufficient time specifically for prayer, during which such consolations might take place. Where some might see such disciplines as stifling God's spirit, Ignatius came to see things in a way that became a foundational principle of the exercises—If we make time for God, God will use that time to speak to us. We needn't seize every opportunity, however. At times, something is more pressing, as in this case, the need for sleep. Indeed, he thought that in cases like this, as strange as it might seem, such opportunities could be the work of the evil spirit.

2 Similar to the way Ignatius identified spiritual consolations as a temptation when they interfered with his studies, he warns against similar temptations when they interfere with sleep and good health. While clearly Ignatius saw spiritual consolation as an aid to the spiritual life, he did not seem to think it always essential to it. Indeed, he thought it more in keeping with the way God works that such consolations should come along sparingly rather than frequently.

3 Since good sleep and bodily health can be used for good or ill, as Ignatius points out, this is all the more reason for those of us who seek virtue and holiness to choose sufficient sleep over additional prayer, which may keep us awake. By being sure to get enough sleep, we can be as equally equipped for good as the less virtuous person might be for evil.

4 As implied in previous excerpts, the peace that comes with overcoming our will and cultivating virtue can help even our bodies to begin to conform themselves to God's will. And this most certainly will contribute to the prevention of the kind of manic thinking, even over prayerful and spiritual topics, that can interrupt sleep.

5 Teresa Rejadell was a Benedictine nun in Barcelona who wrote to Ignatius on numerous occasions asking for spiritual advice.

☐ The Importance of Self-Care

All the rest of the day he spent thinking about the things of God that he had meditated upon or read that day. But when he went to bed, great enlightenment, great spiritual consolations, often came to him; so that they made him lose much of the time he had allotted to sleep, which was not much. Examining this several times, he thought to himself that he had ample time assigned for converse with God,[1] and all the rest of the day as well; and he began to doubt, therefore, whether that enlightenment came from a good spirit. He concluded that it would be better to ignore it and to sleep for the allotted time.

MEMOIRS, 26

The second is something that happens to many people given to prayer or contemplation: because they exercise their minds much, they cannot sleep afterwards because they keep thinking about matters they have contemplated and pictured. Hence, the enemy tries hard to preserve good thoughts so that the body will suffer from the loss of sleep.[2] This must be altogether avoided. With a healthy body you will be able to do much; with a weakened body I am not sure what you will be able to do. A sound body is a great help for doing either much good or much evil: much evil in persons of depraved will and evil habits, much good in persons whose will is entirely given to God our Lord and trained to habits of virtue ...[3] God our Lord requires only that my soul be conformed to his divine majesty; so conformed, it makes the body act in conformity to his divine will,[4] whether we like it or not—wherein is our great struggle, and the good pleasure of the eternal and sovereign goodness.

LETTER TO TERESA REJADELL[5]

6 This is a temptation that many of us find ourselves needing to better avoid. It is easy to neglect the self while doing something to help others. It might even be seen as heroic. But, characteristically, Ignatius encourages moderation and the avoidance of extremes.

7 Ignatius maintained regular correspondence with a number of influential political figures in his day, including members of the nobility like the Borgia family, and civil and religious leaders throughout Europe. This piece of "diplomatic" advice reflects his acquaintance with the ways of politics. At times, Ignatius had to deal with the political tensions that came with Jesuits, for example, being court confessors or tutors in rival kingdoms. He cautioned missionaries to be especially careful in this regard, as often it was impossible to know in advance the political structures and practices of the new cultures they were encountering.

8 Ignatius understood the spirit of obedience as extending beyond the bounds of the Society of Jesus and the church. He often advised Jesuits (as he does here) to treat the judgments of experts in a given field as they would the judgments of their religious superior. This was especially true when such judgments concerned their health and well-being.

9 Francesco Mancini, a Jesuit, was seriously ill at the time this letter was written. When the Jesuit community could not offer him the treatment he needed, Mancini went to stay with his family to receive care. Ignatius wrote Mancini to assure him that despite his absence from the Jesuit community (which he did not desire), his bond with the Society was still strong.

With regard to himself, he should take care not to neglect himself for the sake of helping others.[6] He should be unwilling to commit even the smallest sin for all the spiritual gain that could be had, nor even place himself in danger of such. For this it will help to converse only sparingly and in public with persons from whom he has reason to fear anything.[7] In a general way he should prescind from the outward person and look upon the creature, not as good-looking or attractive, but as someone bathed in the blood of Christ, and image of God, a temple of the Holy Spirit, etc.

LETTER TO THOSE SENT ON MISSIONS

Sickness and Obedience

Therefore consider yourself under obedience in employing any medical remedies and aids that are suggested to you, as well as whatever forms of decent recreation, even physical, may be recommended to you; for in this way you will more speedily get past your present illness with God's help, so that you can dedicate yourself fully to his service.[8] And you should not think that working to recover your health is an insignificant occupation when you desire it for no other purpose than to serve God, and in conformity with God's will.

LETTER TO FRANCESCO MANCINI[9]

1 Ignatius is writing to the religious sister Teresa Rejadell, who seems to be having doubts about the life she has chosen. The questions that he presents as "the obstacles and impediments" that the enemy places before her are essentially the same questions that he struggled with when he first considered the possibility of religious life. Since he was able to overcome these doubts, he seems to be confident that she can, too. We might consider Ignatius's attributing these doubts to the "enemy" as harsh, but it is important to consider that Ignatius believed that once someone made a commitment to religious life, there was no other choice but to persevere. Thus, doubts of this sort would easily be seen as the temptation of the evil spirit. And, indeed, though we might be less inclined to see doubts as evil today, we would certainly discourage anyone prepared to undertake something they thought to be willed by God from being deterred by doubt and uncertainty.

2 Ignatius repeatedly returns to this theme: his belief that the pursuit of personal glory is incompatible with the life dedicated to the service of God. This is not too surprising for the one who describes himself at the beginning of his memoirs as "having a great and foolish desire to win fame" (*Memoirs*, 4).

3 Though she was a laywoman, Ignatius encouraged Isabel Roser to live her life as a Jesuit would. He thus promised her the same thing he promised every Jesuit—that those living such a life should expect and even relish insults and persecution.

☐ Obstacles in the Spiritual Life

Regarding the first point, the enemy's general practice with persons who desire and have begun to serve God our Lord is to bring up obstacles and impediments. This is the first weapon with which he attempts to wound them; namely, "How are you going to live your whole life amid such penance, with no enjoyment from friends, relatives, or possessions, leading such a lonely life and never having any ease? There are other less perilous ways you can save your soul." He suggests that we will have to live a longer life amid all these hardships than any human ever lived. He does not tell us about the great comforts and consolations which our Lord is accustomed to give such persons if the new servant of the Lord breaks through all these obstacles and deliberately chooses to suffer along with his Creator and Lord.[1]

LETTER TO TERESA REJADELL

Insults and Persecution

You mention how many acts of spitefulness, intrigue, and untruthfulness have besieged you on every side. This does not surprise me in the least, even if it were much worse. For at the moment you decide, will, and strive with all your strength for the glory, honor, and service of God our Lord, at that moment you join battle and raise your standard against the world, and prepare yourself to cast away lofty and embrace lowly things, resolving to treat equally the high or the low, honor or dishonor, wealth or poverty, love or hatred, welcome or rejection—in short, the world's glory or all its abuse.... And if our desire is to live absolutely in honor, and our neighbor's esteem, we can never be solidly rooted in God our Lord, nor can we remain unscathed when faced with affronts.[2]

LETTER TO ISABEL ROSER[3]

1 The spiritual discipline of "*agere contra*," or "to act against," is not unique to Ignatius, but it is one he repeatedly advises practicing. Basically, it is overcoming one's worst tendencies and habits in a positive way by making a practice of doing the opposite. For example, someone who is inclined to obsessive overwork would be urged to be more deliberate in taking leisure time, while someone inclined to apathy or indolence should tackle extra tasks.

2 In his initial spiritual zeal, Ignatius found these practices of "mortification" and neglect of the body helpful for keeping his focus on God. As he progressed further in the spiritual life, however, he moderated such practices, especially when they endangered his health and his ministry.

☐ *Agere Contra,* "To Act Against"[1]

Overcoming the Temptations of Desolation

Thirteenth Annotation. The thirteenth: It is likewise to be remarked that, as, in the time of consolation, it is easy and not irksome to be in contemplation the full hour, so it is very hard in the time of desolation to fill it out. For this reason, the person who is exercising himself, in order to act against the desolation and conquer the temptations, ought always to stay somewhat more than the full hour; so as to accustom himself not only to resist the adversary, but even to overthrow him.

THE SPIRITUAL EXERCISES

Letting Go

He begged alms in Manresa every day. He did not eat meat nor drink wine, even though they were offered to him. He did not fast on Sundays, and if they gave him a little wine, he drank it. Because he had been very fastidious in taking care of his hair, as was the fashion at that time (and his was handsome), he decided to let it go its way according to nature without combing or cutting it or covering it with anything by night or day. For the same reason he let the nails grow on toes and fingers because he had been fastidious in this too.[2]

MEMOIRS, 31

⟨∾⟩ In Ignatius's view, *agere contra* is not just a useful principle for helping us to overcome temptations to do evil or immoral things. It also helps us guard against doing the right thing for the wrong reasons. In this way, it also helps us to reorder our motivations by opposing in ourselves inclinations that others might not see in our apparently well-intentioned outward actions.

Desire to Serve God Only

Sixteenth Annotation. The sixteenth: For this—namely, that the Creator and Lord may work more surely in His creature—it is very expedient, if it happens that the soul is attached or inclined to a thing inordinately, that one should move himself, putting forth all his strength, to come to the contrary of what he is wrongly drawn to. Thus if he inclines to seeking and possessing an office or benefice, not for the honor and glory of God our Lord, nor for the spiritual well-being of souls, but for his own temporal advantage and interests, he ought to excite his feelings to the contrary, being instant in prayers and other spiritual exercises, and asking God our Lord for the contrary, namely, not to want such office or benefice, or any other thing, unless His Divine Majesty, putting his desires in order, change his first inclination for him, so that the motive for desiring or having one thing or another be only the service, honor, and glory of His Divine Majesty.

THE SPIRITUAL EXERCISES

1 Since in our own day the word "scruple" itself frequently carries a negative connotation, as an excess of guilt to be altogether avoided, it is important to bear in mind that this is not how Ignatius understands it. He suggests, rather, that "real" scruples can be helpful in the spiritual life; and that even false ones might be an indicator of virtue.

☐ True and False Scruples

First Note. The first: They commonly call a scruple[1] what proceeds from our own judgment and freedom: that is to say, when I freely decide that that is sin which is not sin, as when it happens that after someone has accidentally stepped on a cross of straw, he decides with his own judgment that he has sinned. This is properly an erroneous judgment and not a real scruple.

Second Note. The second: After I have stepped on that cross, or after I have thought or said or done some other thing, there comes to me a thought from without that I have sinned, and on the other hand it appears to me that I have not sinned; still I feel disturbance in this; that is to say, in as much as I doubt and in as much as I do not doubt.

That is a real scruple and temptation which the enemy sets.

Third Note. Third: The first scruple—of the first note—is much to be abhorred, because it is all error; but the second—of the second note—for some space of time is of no little profit to the soul which is giving itself to spiritual exercises; rather in great manner it purifies and cleanses such a soul, separating it much from all appearance of sin: according to that saying of Gregory: "It belongs to good minds to see a fault where there is no fault."

THE SPIRITUAL EXERCISES

2   Ignatius's general confession would have involved a period of reflection on the sins of his past life (and even, in his case, writing them down), ultimately leading to a confession of these sins to a priest who would, by means of the sacrament, offer God's absolution. The "false" scruples from which he suffered were an enduring lack of confidence that his sins had indeed been forgiven.

3   As with Francis Borgia, Ignatius again touts the advantages of having another person help us to make the right decisions regarding our health.

4   In light of the previous note, it is interesting here to witness how Ignatius's understanding of obedience developed. He learned eventually to submit to his confessors' judgment regarding the nature of his sins, and that they were, in fact, forgiven. In Ignatius's understanding of obedience the superior "who holds the place of Christ our Lord" exercises a similar authority with regard to questions of sin as well as matters of discipline and mission.

5   Valentín Marín, a young Jesuit working in Sicily, was known for his academic and preaching talents. He was also known to be overly scrupulous, something that Ignatius tried to address both through Marín's superiors and in this personal letter.

Ridding Oneself of Temptation

But here he began to have much trouble from scruples, for even though the general confession[2] he had made at Montserrat had been quite carefully done and all in writing as has been said, still at times it seemed to him that he had not confessed certain things. This caused him much distress, because although he confessed that, he was not satisfied. Thus he began to look for some spiritual men who could cure him from these scruples, but nothing helped him.

... Although he was practically convinced that those scruples did him much harm and that it would be good to get rid of them, he could not break himself off.

MEMOIRS, 34

Benefits and Dangers

Scrupulosity, up to a certain point, is usually not harmful as long as it makes a person be more vigilant and careful about avoiding offenses against God while at the same time refraining from any judgment that this or that is a sin (even though he suspects or fears it might be), and so long as he relies on the judgment of some person whom he ought to trust, setting aside his own judgment and accepting this person's opinion.[3] Without these two aids, a scrupulous person runs the gravest risk of offending God by not avoiding what he thinks is sinful (though it is not), as well as of losing occasions and ability to serve him—or even his natural good judgment.

And so, Master Marín, determine to keep fixed in your mind these two resolutions: first, not to form a judgment or personal determination that something is sinful when it is not clearly such and is ordinarily not considered such by others; second, even when you are very fearful that something is a sin, to submit to the judgment of your superior ... who holds the place of Christ our Lord.[4]

LETTER TO VALENTÍN MARÍN[5]

6 As much as Ignatius advises against temptations to vanity, he is equally emphatic about avoiding the contrary temptation to false humility. One must recognize rather than undervalue the gifts he or she has been given by God, so that they might properly be put to use in God's service. "Humility" is not a virtue if it leads to self-deprecation and the failure to recognize and make use of our God-given talents.

Discernment of Scruples

In this way the Lord deigned that he awake as from sleep. As he now had some experience of the diversity of spirits from the lessons God had given him, he began to examine the means by which that spirit had come. He thus decided with great lucidity not to confess anything from the past any more; and so from that day forward he remained free of those scruples and held it for certain that Our Lord had mercifully deigned to deliver him.

MEMOIRS, 37

Overcoming False Scruples

When such good soul wants to speak or do something within the Church, within the understanding of our Superiors, and which should be for the glory of God our Lord, and there comes to him a thought or temptation from without that he should neither say nor do that thing—bringing to him apparent reasons of vainglory[6] or of another thing, etc.,—then he ought to raise his understanding to his Creator and Lord, and if he sees that it is His due service, or at the least not contrary to it, he ought to act diametrically against such temptation, according to St. Bernard, answering the same: "Neither for thee did I begin, nor for thee will I stop."

THE SPIRITUAL EXERCISES

Part 6
Living with and
for Others

1 Here again Ignatius speaks to intention and motivation. When we are engaged in the service of others, we must be conscious of how our penitential practices might affect our fitness and our ability to serve them—as much, if not more than, how they might offer us personal spiritual benefit.

2 Arnold van Hees was a young Jesuit who, at the time of the composition of this letter, was traveling to Cologne, Germany, to complete his studies and help establish a Jesuit community there.

3 We see here how in Ignatius's past experience his growing awareness of his impact on others caused him to moderate some of his extreme practices, such as neglecting his personal grooming.

☐ Self-Care and Moderation

Moderation has staying power; what puts excessive strain on the body cannot last. Understand, then, that Father General's mind on this matter is that, in whatever spiritual, academic, or even bodily exertions you undertake, your charity should be guided by the rule of discretion; that you should safeguard the health of your own body in order to aid your neighbors' souls;[1] and that in this matter each of you should look out for the other, indeed, for both of you.

LETTER TO ARNOLD VAN HEES[2]

At Manresa too, where he stayed almost a year, after he began to be consoled by God, and saw the fruit which he bore in dealing with souls, he gave up those extremes he had formerly practiced, and he now cut his nails and his hair.[3]

MEMOIRS, 41

4 Taking things a step further, Ignatius challenges us to consider how our good treatment of others might guide how we should treat ourselves.

5 Knowing personally how excessive zeal in mortifications and penances could endanger one's health, Ignatius's tendency became to insist on moderation. Still, he saw that such practices could be valuable for certain individuals in certain situations. To guard against abuse, he suggests here that such austerity should not be undertaken without the supervision of another.

6 This is a lengthy instruction that includes much advice and encouragement that proved helpful for the Jesuits of the time, and from which all believers today can still benefit. Because of its length and depth of insight, it is excerpted numerous times in this book. Addressed to the community at a Jesuit seminary in Portugal that was flourishing with numerous "scholastics" (Jesuits in training who have not yet made their final vows), one of the concerns of the letter was to address what some saw as an unhealthy excess of zeal in this community.

7 These are general principles that we could all do well to pay attention to. We attend to our health not only for our own well-being but also so that we may continue our good work.

8 Gaspar Berze, working with Francis Xavier, was a successful missionary to India. When Xavier set out to extend the mission to Japan and China, Berze replaced him as superior of the Indian mission. Berze was a hard worker known to neglect his health at times. Unfortunately, by the time this letter reached India, Berze had already died.

Treat Yourself with Equal Charity

Your Reverence has been somewhat faulted by Father Don Antonio [de Cordoba] for your treatment of your own person; and from other quarters also we understand that you do not treat yourself—your body, I mean—with the same charity you show toward others.[4] You eat badly, overwork, and you do not let others assist you. Consequently, in view of the special charity shown by Father Don Antonio in this regard, Our Father is placing him in charge of Your Reverence's treatment of your body.[5]

LETTER TO FRANCIS BORGIA

While it is dangerous to sail a vessel empty, since it will be tossed about by temptations, it is even more dangerous to load it so heavily that it sinks.

LETTER TO THE FATHERS AND SCHOLASTICS AT COIMBRA

Set a Good Example[6]

There are two dangers in treating yourself so harshly. The first is that, barring a miracle, Your Reverence will not be able to last very long in the holy ministries you undertake. Rather, you will either be cut off by death or become too ill to continue your labors, which it is reckoned would impede great service of God and help of his souls, in which you could employ yourself for many years in good health. The second danger is that, being so hard on yourself, you could easily become too hard on those under you; if only by your example, you might push others to excessive effort—the more so the better they are.[7]

LETTER TO GASPAR BERZE[8]

~ This is good advice because we can put a lot of pressure on ourselves to appear truly compassionate or sensitive—for instance, in the form of tears. This, however, is another instance in which Ignatius urges us to recognize that God works in different ways in different people. Indeed, Ignatius seems to have had specific people in mind for whom he believes that tears would be a hindrance rather than a help to their feelings of compassion and charitable actions. One of the challenges of the spiritual life is becoming aware of how God moves each of us uniquely, and being content with how that manifests itself according to God's will, rather than jealous that God is moving someone else in a way that we might find more desirable or acceptable.

1 Nicholas Floris (*Goudanus* indicates that he was from Gouda) was a Jesuit who zealously and successfully went about his ministry, but was disturbed by spiritual dryness and an absence of the gift of tears like those asked for in the grace of the third week. In this letter, Ignatius tries to allay his concerns, assuring him that this gift is not essential to the spiritual life.

☐ Compassion

When someone feels compassion for the miseries of the neighbor in the will and the higher part of his soul, desires to do what he can to relieve them, and performs the offices of a person who has this active will for taking the necessary means, he needs no further tears or sensible feelings in the heart. While some people may have tears because their nature is such that the affections in the higher part of their souls easily overflow into the lower, or because God our Lord, seeing that it would be good for them, grants them to melt into tears, this still does not mean that they have greater charity or accomplish more than other persons who are without tears but have no less strong affections in the higher part of the soul, that is, a strong and efficacious willing (which is the proper act of charity) of God's service and the good of souls, just like that of persons who have abundant tears. Moreover, I would tell Your Reverence something of which I am convinced: There are persons to whom I would not give the gift of tears even if it were in my power to do so, because it does not help their charity and damages their heads and bodies, and consequently hinders any practice of charity. So Your Reverence ought not to be distressed over the lack of external tears; keep your will strong and good and show it in your actions, and that will suffice for your own perfection, the help of others, and the service of God.

LETTER TO NICHOLAS FLORIS (GOUDANUS)[1]

1 Here Ignatius advises us to beware of hasty decisions. He is speaking of twin dangers. Either someone making the exercises might, while experiencing consolation, too hastily make an irrevocable life decision, or his or her spiritual director might unduly influence the enthusiastic retreatant toward a decision that the director finds desirable, such as a commitment to vowed religious life.

2 Ignatius encouraged and himself employed a similar wisdom with regard to admitting men to the Jesuits. Enthusiasm and even sincere desire were not enough if the inquirer did not have the talents (e.g., the ability to complete the required studies) and strength of character to persevere in Jesuit life.

☐ Guiding Others

Fourteenth Annotation. The fourteenth: If he who is giving the Exercises sees that he who is receiving them is going on in consolation and with much fervor, he ought to warn him not to make any inconsiderate and hasty promise or vow:[1] and the more light of character he knows him to be, the more he ought to warn and admonish him. For, though one may justly influence another to embrace the religious life, in which he is understood to make vows of obedience, poverty and chastity, and, although a good work done under vow is more meritorious than one done without it, one should carefully consider the circumstances and personal qualities of the individual and how much help or hindrance he is likely to find in fulfilling the thing he would want to promise.[2]

THE SPIRITUAL EXERCISES

1 It is significant to note that Ignatius thought it permissible to influence people to take up religious life in our everyday encounters with them, but not when directing them through the exercises. It underscores his belief that the spiritual exercises provided a privileged and more direct encounter with God, in which we are more open to God's communication as well as more vulnerable to suggestion. Both the retreatant and the director must share in this belief, so that the former may trust God to guide them personally and the latter might avoid the temptation to impose their desires, preferences, or opinions. The spiritual director must observe this delicate balance.

2 This sentence offers perhaps the best brief description of Ignatius's ideal spiritual director—the guide who can most successfully avoid getting in the way of what God is doing. As the most experienced spiritual directors recognize, this is not as easy as it might seem. The same hazards that one can encounter in therapeutic relationships, such as projection, transference, and sexual attraction, can also interfere with the relationship between spiritual director and directee. At times, then, if one of these or similar dynamics becomes an obstacle, termination of the spiritual direction relationship might be necessary to letting God work.

3 Though this is not an enforced silence like that of the exercises, Ignatius suggests here how a certain amount of silence and restraint can be helpful in preparing us to share our experience of God with others in our everyday encounters.

☐ Letting God Do the Work

Fifteenth Annotation. The fifteenth: He who is giving the Exercises ought not to influence him who is receiving them more to poverty or to a promise, than to their opposites, nor more to one state or way of life than to another. For though, outside the Exercises,[1] we can lawfully and with merit influence everyone who is probably fit to choose continence, virginity, the religious life, and all manner of evangelical perfection, still in the Spiritual Exercises, when seeking the Divine Will, it is more fitting and much better, that the Creator and Lord Himself should communicate Himself to His devout soul, inflaming it with His love and praise, and disposing it for the way in which it will be better able to serve Him in future. So, he who is giving the Exercises should not turn or incline to one side or the other, but standing in the centre like a balance, leave the Creator to act immediately with the creature, and the creature with its Creator and Lord.[2]

THE SPIRITUAL EXERCISES

Listen First

Ever since Manresa the pilgrim had the habit when he ate with anyone, never to speak at table except to answer briefly; but he listened to what was said and noted some things which he took as the occasion to speak about God, and when the meal was finished, he did so.[3]

MEMOIRS, 57

1 This practice is in many ways similar to that of Saint Paul in his first letter to the Corinthians and was likely influenced by it: "For though I am free with respect to all, I have made myself a slave to all, so that I might win more of them…. To the weak I became weak, so that I might win the weak. I have become all things to all people, so that I might by any means save some" (1 Corinthians 9:19–22).

2 This is another instance where we can see why Ignatius places so much emphasis on understanding the movements of various spirits. If we understand how the evil spirit works to win us over to evil, we often find that we can use the same—or similar—strategy to lead them to God.

3 In one of the earliest papal missions Alfonso Salmerón and Paschase Broët, two Jesuit priests involved in the founding of the Society of Jesus, were sent as papal delegates to Ireland to help with problems in the church brought about by Henry VIII's break with Rome. Ignatius sent the two a series of letters with detailed instructions for both their dangerous journey and how they were to proceed once they arrived.

☐ "Go in Their Door"

In any conversation where we are trying to win a person over and ensnare him for the greater service of God our Lord, we should adopt the same procedure the enemy uses with a good soul—he always for evil and we always for good. The enemy enters through the other's door and comes out his own. He enters the other's door by praising rather than contradicting his ways; he cultivates familiarity with the soul by drawing it to good and holy thoughts that bring the good soul calm. Then, little by little, he endeavors to come out his own door, drawing the person under the appearance of good to some harmful error or illusion, always for evil. In the same way, we [acting] for good, can praise a person or go along with him on some particular good point, passing over in silence any bad points he might have.[1] Once we have won his love, we will better get what we want. Thus, we go in his door and come out our own.[2]

LETTER TO ALFONSO SALMERÓN AND PASCHASE BROËT[3]

⟨∽⟩ It is not hard to see that this encouragement to treat opponents with charity also serves as a helpful approach in our everyday lives, especially when we encounter those with whom we disagree.

1 This advice serves as an excellent "examination of conscience" for one who is considering whether to admonish another. Helpfully, Ignatius emphasizes that one not see such correction as an obligation or duty which *must* be performed. Instead, one should consider the likelihood of success and whether it might be imprudent or even harmful for a given person to attempt it.

2 Antonio Brandão was a Portuguese scholastic who posed a series of questions to Ignatius regarding the life of a scholastic. These included how to live alongside other scholastics and in relationship with one's superiors in the Jesuit order—principally one's immediate local superior, but also those individuals delegated to supervise specific activities of the community or operations of the house. Though originally Ignatius's letter was a specific response to Brandão's questions, it was published more widely for the benefit of other scholastics as well.

☐ Love's Authority

In order that both he who is giving the Spiritual Exercises, and he who is receiving them, may more help and benefit themselves, let it be presupposed that every good Christian is to be more ready to save his neighbor's proposition than to condemn it. If he cannot save it, let him inquire how he means it; and if he means it badly, let him correct him with charity. If that is not enough, let him seek all the suitable means to bring him to mean it well, and save himself.

THE SPIRITUAL EXERCISES

Success in this matter depends largely upon the authority enjoyed by the person giving the correction, or upon his love and the perception of this love. Lacking either of these, the correction will produce no effect of amendment. Correcting others is thus not for everybody. Moreover, no matter how a person gives an admonition, deeming that it will lead to the person's amendment, it is better not to state things too forthrightly, but indirectly under some pretext; for one sin can engender another—the sin originally committed may incline a person not to accept the alms of correction well.[1]

LETTER TO ANTONIO BRANDÃO[2]

3 During his lifetime, Ignatius made one significant exception regarding the rule that Jesuits were not to become bishops. Having offered the services of the Jesuits to help reinvigorate the church in Ethiopia, he was asked to make one of his men available to become the new patriarch of the region. Despite both their reservations, he asked João Nunes Barreto, already an experienced African missionary, to accept the position. Barreto took consolation in the fact that he did not aspire to the position, but accepted it only out of obedience. Ignatius wrote him several letters of support and advice during the course of his ministry in Ethiopia.

4 Ignatius's writings demonstrate a variety of attitudes toward the Protestant Christians of his day. Certainly, he believed them to be in error. But, as in most other similar situations, he tends to encourage a more diplomatic approach when dealing with them. Some Jesuits were actively engaged in efforts to draw Protestants back into the Catholic fold and did so with Ignatius's encouragement and support. However, Ignatius often seems more concerned with the conversion of non-Christians than he was with the "re-conversion" of Protestant Christians. That said, Ignatius could still use harsh words when speaking of the Protestant "heretics."

5 The Jesuits addressed were leaving for Germany in response to a request of the duke of Bavaria for professors of theology. Alfonso Salmerón, Claude Jay, and Peter Canisius were sent to serve in this capacity at the University of Ingolstadt. Ignatius insisted that they also engage in the full range of Jesuit ministries, which included the founding of a Jesuit college. Peter Canisius, considered a saint by the Catholic Church, had an especially profound impact in Germany, eventually leading many Germans back to the Catholic church by means of his scholarship, preaching, and popular catechisms.

Concentrate on the abuses or disorders that can be corrected gently and in a way that makes the need for reform evident to the people there; begin with these, and you will gain authority for reforming other abuses.

LETTER TO JOÃO NUNES BARRETO[3]

Dealing with Heretics

You should attempt to win the friendship of any leading adversaries and of the more influential among those who are heretics, or suspected of heresy, and are not altogether obdurate. You should try to withdraw them from their error tactfully and lovingly.[4]

LETTER TO JESUITS LEAVING FOR GERMANY[5]

1 While probably not meant as a criticism of monastic life, this statement does in some ways reflect the shift in the understanding of religious life that Ignatius's Society of Jesus represented, placing as much emphasis on ministry and works of charity as it did on preaching and prayer.

2 This is one of the primary underlying assumptions of *The Spiritual Exercises*. The practical outcome of the exercises (and, indeed, Ignatian spirituality as a whole) is that they should inspire those participating in them (both director and retreatant) to share their gifts with others in concrete actions.

3 Ignatius experienced deeply the kind of mutual love he describes in his relationship with Saint Francis Xavier, perhaps his closest friend. When a Jesuit being sent to India fell ill, Ignatius sent Xavier in his place. Though the two corresponded regularly (as much as the circumstances of the time allowed), they would never see each other again.

4 Here we see further reason why Ignatius insisted on so much written correspondence by members of the Society. Not only did it promote awareness of the work of the Jesuits worldwide, it also strengthened bonds between them, allowing them to be more successful.

5 These words of support were written to Diego Miró, the embattled second provincial of Portugal, as he tried to deal with the contentious situation surrounding differences of opinion regarding his predecessor, Simão Rodrigues. Eventually, matters became so serious that Ignatius sent Miró a letter authorizing him to dismiss Rodrigues from the Society if he failed to report to Rome, as Ignatius had requested. Miró was spared the task of dismissing Rodrigues, one of the co-founders of the Jesuits, by the fact that Rodrigues was already on his way to Rome when the letter arrived.

☐ Mutual Love and the Common Good

First, it is well to remark two things: the first is that love ought to be put more in deeds than in words.[1] The second, love consists in interchange between the two parties; that is to say in the lover's giving and communicating to the beloved what he has or out of what he has or can; and so, on the contrary, the beloved to the lover. So that if the one has knowledge, he give to the one who has it not. The same of honors, of riches; and so the one to the other.[2]

THE SPIRITUAL EXERCISES

The third is mutual love, which by nature cools with distance and forgetfulness and, contrariwise, is preserved and quickened by remembrance, which supplies for actual presence.[3] For among persons who are normally absent from one another as our men are, it is clear how essential it is for them to refresh their memory of one another in order to keep up their love. The same effect is had by the charity shown by the one writing, which, as it creates an obligation, also helps to love.[4]

LETTER TO THE ENTIRE SOCIETY

Don't Be Swayed By Criticism

You should not allow any considerations or talk from the crowd to keep you from what could turn out to be of great service to God and to Their Highnesses and for the common good.

LETTER TO DIEGO MIRÓ[5]

1 This piece of advice in the exercises would seem to rise out of Ignatius's previously described practice of limiting his speech. The fewer "idle" words that we engage in, the less likely we are to lose focus on more important spiritual matters.

2 Among the foremost concerns of the spiritual conversation in which Ignatius the pilgrim and his companions engaged others was distinguishing between mortal and venial sins. This caused concern among authorities in the Inquisition, as Ignatius explains in his *Memoirs*: "After twenty-two days of imprisonment, they were summoned to hear the sentence, which was that no error was found in their life or teaching. Therefore, they could do what they had been doing, teaching doctrine and speaking about the things of God, so long as they never defined: this is a mortal sin or this is venial, until they had spent four years in further study" (102). These passages demonstrate Ignatius's continuing concern with such distinctions between serious (mortal) and lesser (venial) sins, especially when one's words or actions might cause serious harm to another.

3 Because of scandals over women's fashion in Venice, only select older priests were allowed to hear ladies' confessions. Azzolini was the one Jesuit who heard such confessions. However, as a confessor he lacked confidence, which at times caused him to be too harsh. Ignatius urges him to consider that since their dress, however scandalous, was a result of conformity to fashion and not an intention to sin, the seriousness of the sin was diminished.

4 The Inquisition in Venice had forbidden any priest under thirty-six years of age from hearing women's confessions. Though Jesuits were authorized by the pope to hear anyone's confession, Ignatius thought it prudent that Jesuits too should conform to the rule rather than cause a stir. Alberto Azzolini, being the only Jesuit priest in Venice beyond that age, was thus given the task of hearing the confession of any woman who desired to confess to a Jesuit.

☐ Judging Others

Be Wary of Idle Words

One must not speak an idle word. By idle word I mean one which does not benefit either me or another, and is not directed to that intention.[1] Hence words spoken for any useful purpose, or meant to profit one's own or another's soul, the body or temporal goods, are never idle, not even if one were to speak of something foreign to one's state of life, as, for instance, if a religious speaks of wars or articles of trade; but in all that is said there is merit in directing well, and sin in directing badly, or in speaking idly.

Nothing must be said to injure another's character or to find fault, because if I reveal a mortal sin that is not public, I sin mortally; if a venial sin, venially; and if a defect, I show a defect of my own.[2]

THE SPIRITUAL EXERCISES

Putting Sin In Context

From a letter of Father Rector we learn that Your Reverence is uneasy about the practice of women in Venice in matters of dress and personal adornment—and rightly so, for they give occasion (which others frequently take) to offend God our Lord. However, where the practice is general and there neither appears to be nor is there any going beyond the usual custom in the matter itself, nor any intention of sinning or leading others to sin, it is not considered mortally sinful.[3]

LETTER TO ALBERTO AZZOLINI[4]

1 This letter gives us a privileged insight into Ignatius's own discernment and decision-making process. This being a matter of such importance, involving legitimate but conflicting demands of obedience and authority, Ignatius resists the temptation to presume that his first reaction is the correct one. Instead he enters into a three-day process of discerning God's will, which includes asking the prayers of others and paying attention to his various interior movements. This, we might be surprised to note, even includes a period of time in which Ignatius seems to doubt his capacity to know God's will. However, his efforts pay off and he is certain that his first inclination was indeed the right one, for to proceed any differently in this matter would be contrary to God's will. Clearly, in the day-to-day business of the Society, Ignatius would not have had such time to consider most of his decisions in this way. He would have to be confident that in most cases his decisions would reflect God's will. But he was known to deliberate at greater length about those things he considered among his most important and weighty decisions, like this one. While we might not approach our decisions with the same intensity, we can take a cue from Ignatius to give sufficient time and prayer, seeking the help and prayers of others, to the more important decisions of our lives.

☐ Conflicting Demands

In the matter of the cardinal's hat, I thought I would give some account to you, as if to my own soul, regarding what took place within me, for God's greater glory. As soon as I learned for certain that the emperor had nominated you and that the Pope was willing to make you a cardinal, I immediately had this impulse or spiritual movement to oppose it in any way I could. However, being unsure of God's will because of the many reasons that occurred to me on both sides, I ordered all the priests in the community to say mass and those not priests to offer their prayers for three days that I might be guided wholly to God's greater glory. Over this period of three days, there were times when, as I reflected and conferred about the matter, I experienced certain fears, or a lack of freedom of spirit for speaking out and opposing it. I thought, "How do I know what God our Lord wants to do?" and did not find in myself total certainty about opposing it. At other times, when I went to my regular prayers, I felt within myself that these fears receded. Repeating this petition at intervals, sometimes with this fear and sometimes with the opposite, I finally found myself, during my regular prayer on the third day and continually thereafter, with a judgment so complete and a will so calm and free to do all I could with the Pope and the cardinals to oppose it that if I failed to do so, I would be, and am, quite certain that I could give no good account of myself to God our Lord, but instead a wholly bad one.[1]

(continued on page 185)

2 This remarkable insight comes in a context that reveals much about Ignatius's vision for the Society of Jesus, and how seriously he took discernment. Francis Borgia was a member of one of Europe's most prominent families and a Jesuit priest. This letter was prompted by the fact that, because of Borgia's status, the emperor had asked the pope to make Borgia a cardinal. This put Ignatius in a difficult position, for he was quite adamant that Jesuits not be made bishops. Yet, Jesuits also took an additional vow of obedience to the pope, which would make it difficult for Ignatius to oppose him should the latter grant the emperor's request. It is with regard to this situation that Ignatius is writing to Borgia, after he had spent three days discerning whether he could support such a decision. As he indicates, Ignatius emerged from this time of discernment still firmly opposed, but he also realized that this needn't be seen as God's final word. The Holy Spirit, he believed, might very well move another to act in a seemingly contradictory manner by insisting on the conferral of the cardinal's position on Borgia. After some deliberation of his own, Borgia came to the same conclusion as Ignatius, making it clear that he would attempt to refuse the honor, if it were to be offered. Ignatius's insight seems especially useful in times like today when different factions in the church engage in quarrels over who represents the faith authentically. Many failures could be avoided simply by recognizing, like Ignatius, that for mysterious reasons God might lead two individuals, or groups of individuals, to seemingly contradictory conclusions, especially if both sides were committed to undertaking the requisite discernment.

However, I held then and I hold now that there would be no contradiction in its being God's will for me to take this course while others take a different one and the dignity be conferred on you. The same divine Spirit could move me to this course for one set of reasons and move others to the opposite for different ones, with the outcome being what the Emperor indicated. May God our Lord act everywhere as may be always for his greater praise and glory.[2]

LETTER TO FRANCIS BORGIA

1 In Ignatius's vision, obedience was not only a holy virtue and an aid to the efficient operation of the Society; it also forged a bond of trust, friendship, and brotherhood. This helps to explain why he would prescribe obedience in a situation like this, when it would seem unnecessary and superfluous.

2 Jesuit obedience was not completely "blind." Ignatius encouraged a process known as "representation," whereby one can present reasons why obedience to a given instruction might not be possible, healthy, or prudent. This, however, had to be done in the correct manner and in the proper spirit. In this letter, Ignatius is reminding Giovanni Battista Viola of this, since it has come to light that this is *not* how he is practicing obedience. Viola was a Jesuit scholastic who drew Ignatius's ire when he got into academic difficulty as a result of not following directions given by Ignatius himself. In this letter, Ignatius is clearly angry and reminds Viola of his obligation of obedience and how it should be understood.

☐ Obedience

Wherever there are any members of the Society, even if only two, one should observe obedience toward the other.[1]

LETTER FOR THE JESUIT SUPERIOR IN ETHIOPIA REGARDING ETHIOPIAN AFFAIRS

Blind Obedience

Now inasmuch as it seems to me that obedience seeks to be blind, I understand blind in two ways: (1) An inferior ought to surrender his own understanding (where there is no question of sin) and do what is commanded him; and (2) an inferior who is or has been given a command by the superior and perceives reasons against what is commanded or drawbacks in it ought humbly to represent to the superior the reasons or drawbacks that occur to him, without attempting to draw him to one side or the other, and afterwards tranquilly to follow the way that is pointed out to him or commanded.[2]

LETTER TO GIOVANNI BATTISTA VIOLA

1 The Jesuit was always to recognize that even in presenting concerns or objections, he must remember that the superior still holds the place of God. Thus, he was not to be presumptuous by implying that he knew better than his superior about a matter of obedience.

2 Ignatius encouraged a proper attitude of obedience not only with one's religious superiors but also with others who might be in authority over Jesuits. For example, if a Jesuit was assigned to work in the kitchen with a cook who was not a Jesuit, he would be expected to obey the cook as if he were his religious superior.

3 As would later be true with many Jesuits, Ignatius often found it more difficult to generate enthusiasm for his studies than for his ministry. Here he uses his imagination to impose a relationship of obedience not unlike the one he would later establish in the Society between the Jesuit in studies and his formation superior.

4 Obedience was above all a means of unity. Some have complained that Ignatius didn't write sufficiently about how to live together in community; this quote and the next suggest a reason for that. For Ignatius, the bond of community is obedience. This can be seen in the decision of Ignatius and his first companions to form the Jesuits. They determined that to stay together as a community of friends it would be necessary to vow obedience to one of their number. That responsibility fell to Ignatius despite his initial refusal and his demand that they vote a second time.

5 This letter was written to the Jesuit scholastics in Gandia, one of the first Jesuit communities in Spain. Since the Constitutions of the Society of Jesus had not yet been published, Ignatius felt the need to explain to them how certain things were to be done. This was his first major letter on obedience, which laid some of the groundwork for his more extensive instruction on obedience during the crisis in Portugal.

☐ Obedience in Community

After having organized and though out the matter, he should present it and say, "I thought this point over personally (or with others, as the case may be), and I wondered (or we gave thought to) whether it might be good this way or that way." In dealing with a superior, he should never say, "It is, or will be, good this way." Instead, he should put it conditionally, asking "whether it is, or will be, good."[1]

INSTRUCTION: PROCEDURE FOR DEALING WITH ANY SUPERIOR[2]

He found great consolation in the following reflection and resolution which he entertained, imagining that the master would be Christ, that one of the students he would call St. Peter and another St. John, and so with each one of the apostles: "When the master orders me, I will think that Christ orders me; when another orders me, I will think that St. Peter orders me."[3]

MEMOIRS, 111

Apart from all these spiritual advantages applicable mainly to individuals, this way of living is essential for the preservation of the entire body of your community. For it is a fact that no group can be preserved as a single body without being united, or be united without order, or have order without a single head to which all the other members are subject in obedience. Hence, if you wish our community to be preserved in being, you must necessarily wish to have someone as your head.[4]

LETTER TO THE JESUITS OF GANDIA[5]

6 Ignatius saw obedience as a means for one to do what all who follow Jesus should do—to put one's entire will at the disposal of God. Thus, his analogy to martyrdom tries to emphasize the fact that as heroic and meritorious as it is to be willing to die for our faith, obedience is putting our entire selves, the whole of our lives, at the service of God. The sacrifice of martyrdom is but one potential consequence of this complete giving over of ourselves to the will of God.

7 Obedience is a means by which God can work through us. The very fact that we know we are doing it for God allows us to succeed in ways we may not if doing something only out of self-love or self-interest. This might be likened to the approach to overcoming addiction that is practiced by twelve-step programs, in which participants admit that they cannot achieve their goal of sobriety on their own but only with the help of a higher power outside themselves.

A Kind of Martyrdom

Without doubt it is a very straight road when a person practices subjugation of his own judgment and will by means of holy obedience; this advantage, however, would be forfeited if the superior were far off. Likewise, this way of life is singularly meritorious for those who know how to make the most of it, for it is a kind of martyrdom which continually cuts off the head of our own judgment and will, putting in place of our own that of Christ our Lord as made known through his minister. And unlike martyrdom, it does not just cut off a single will—the will to live—but all our wills together.[6]

LETTER TO THE JESUITS OF GANDIA

For we see from experience that men of average or even below-average talent are often instruments of remarkable and supernatural achievements, because they are completely obedient and through this virtue allow themselves to be moved and possessed by the mighty hand of the Author of all good. Conversely, we see great talents laboring harder without achieving even average results; the reason is that, being moved by themselves—that is, by their own self-love—or at least not letting themselves be properly moved by God our Lord through obedience to their superiors, they produce results that are proportionate, not to the almighty hand of God our Lord, who does not accept them as his instruments, but instead to their own weak and feeble hands.[7]

LETTER TO DIEGO MIRÓ

1 Unlike the three kinds of humility, which are discussed in the next chapter, Ignatius believed that the first degree of obedience was by itself insufficient. Simply doing what we are told is not enough. The Jesuit and the Christian ought to grow into at least the second degree of obedience and should strive to attain the third.

2 The greatest exercise of our free will, from Ignatius's point of view, is giving it over to the God who gave it to us. This kind of exchange is similar to that prayed for in the "Take Lord, Receive" prayer that concludes the exercises.

3 The third degree of obedience for Jesuits involves this complete submission to the superior's will, not only obeying, but making the will and understanding of the superior his own. We all can practice this third degree of obedience, however, by ardently seeking God's will and making that will our own, especially when it challenges our own selfish desires.

4 This reflects Ignatius's strong belief that if Jesuits sincerely sought God's will, they could be confident that God's will and the superior's will were one and the same.

5 Giovanni Battista Guidini was a Jesuit brother who was expressing a desire to become a priest. In consultation with Guidini's superior, Ignatius determined that Guidini did not have the competency to complete the requisite studies. Ignatius sternly writes that given the circumstances, this is clearly a temptation, and that Guidini should be content continuing to pursue the vocation to which he was more properly called. This is another place we see Ignatius's more practical side at work. It is Guidini's deficiencies when it came to studies that convinces Ignatius that this is a temptation, and not necessarily some deep spiritual insight.

☐ Degrees of Obedience

I also desire it to be firmly fixed in your souls that the first degree of obedience, which consists in the execution of what is commanded, is quite low. It does not deserve the name of obedience[1] or attain the worth of this virtue unless it rises to the second degree, which consists in making the superior's will one's own, in such a way that there is not just effective execution but a conformity of wish, an identical willing and not willing ... Think it no small fruit of your free will that you are able to restore it totally in obedience to the one who gave it to you. In this you do not lose it; instead, you perfect it, wholly conforming your own to the most certain rule of all rectitude, God's own will[2] ... But whoever aims at making a complete and perfect oblation of himself must, in addition to his will, offer his understanding. This is the further and the highest degree of obedience. He must not only have the same will as the superior but also be of the same mind as he, submitting his own judgment to the superior's to the extent that a devoted will is able to influence the understanding.[3]

LETTER TO JESUITS IN PORTUGAL

God's Way

Finally, Giovanni Battista, if you have given all to God, allow yourself to be guided by God; act not in your own way but in God's way. And this way you are to learn by obedience to your superior.[4]

LETTER TO GIOVANNI BATTISTA GUIDINI[5]

1 Ignatius knew that the work of missionaries, like that of the early apostles and saints, often took place in a state of flux and incompleteness. He encourages the missionary to be focused on his work, with an eye to completion. While it is true that a missionary's ultimate achievement might only be to get things started, Ignatius wanted missionary Jesuits to set a higher goal even though they may never reach it. Setting such goals also gave the missionaries something to inspire them under less than ideal circumstances.

2 Ignatius offers especially practical advice for one busily engaged in ministry—do what you can and should do, and ask others for help with the rest. As the number of Jesuits available for Jesuit ministries has diminished in recent decades, this is an especially important practice for ensuring the future of their most important ministries.

3 Fulvio Androzzi was already a priest when he entered the Society of Jesus and thus set to work early in his Jesuit career. He was one of the Jesuits' first spiritual writers. He was very successful in a variety of ministries, no doubt more so thanks to the encouragement and advice he received from Ignatius.

☐ Setting Priorities

He should consider which religious works he spends his time on. He should prefer before any others those for which he is specifically sent. Among other works, he should prefer those which are better—that is, the spiritual over the corporal, the more urgent over the less urgent, the universal over the particular, the permanent and lasting over those that do not last, etc.—in cases where he cannot do both. He should also remember that it is not enough to get a good and religious work started: he must as far as possible complete it and put it on a permanent footing.[1]

Letter to Those Sent on Missions

Advice for the Busy

When you are very busy, you need to make a choice and devote your efforts to the more important occupations, that is, those in which there is a greater service of God, greater spiritual advantage for the neighbor, more universal or perfect good, etc. Reserving a little time to organize yourself and your own activities will also be a considerable help for this. If there are people from the area who could take your place in some matters, it would be good to share some of the labor with them so as to be free for more important matters. Thus, it would be good for someone else to take charge of the processions you mention; they are not all that appropriate to our way of proceeding, although it is a fine thing that in order to get this holy practice launched, you started it off and gave the example to the others.[2]

Letter to Fulvio Androzzi[3]

4 These specific suggestions were the kind of charitable organizations that the Jesuits, other religious orders, and confraternities (organizations of laypersons dedicated to a certain cause, devotion, or saint) were opening or supporting at the time. The Jesuits, for example, operated a home for former prostitutes for a time, until the fear of scandal, real or imagined, prompted them to turn the work over to others.

5 While Ignatius was not opposed to penances and devotional practices, which he himself was known to practice, he frequently encouraged Jesuits, as he does here, to give priority to charitable works done in the service of others.

Charitable Works Superior to Fasts

Since our men need to reduce people's esteem for corporal penances, which they esteem and practice to excess, you ought to set charity before them by word and example. For this it would be good to have hospitals available for pilgrims and for the sick, both curable and incurable; to give and get others to give private and public alms to the poor; to help marry orphan girls; and to start confraternities for redeeming captives and rearing abandoned boys and girls, etc.[4] This would let the people see in a tangible way works that are superior to their fasts, etc.[5]

LETTER TO JOÃO NUNES BARRETO

Part 7
Imitating Jesus

1 The "Kingdom Prayer" begins the second week of *The Spiritual Exercises*, which focuses on the contemplation of the life of Jesus from his birth until the eve of his betrayal, trial, and death. It seems a radical place to begin, asking Jesus for the grace to imitate him in "injury" and poverty. However, Ignatius does qualify it by saying, "if only it be Thy greater service and praise," an indication that not all would be called to serve God in this way. For Ignatius, however, the ideal life was the one lived most in conformity with the life of Jesus, especially sharing in his material and spiritual poverty and experiencing similar suffering and persecution. And this was the ideal that he set before those who would pray the exercises, knowing still that only a small percentage would actually be called to such a radical following of Jesus. Therefore this particular prayer serves as an opportunity for us to express this radical desire sincerely, and in that context to determine to what extent God wills us to approach or achieve this ideal.

☐ The "Kingdom Prayer"

Those who will want to be more devoted and signalize themselves in all service of their King Eternal and universal Lord, not only will offer their persons to the labor, but even, acting against their own sensuality and against their carnal and worldly love, will make offerings of greater value and greater importance, saying: "Eternal Lord of all things, I make my oblation with Thy favor and help, in presence of Thy infinite Goodness and in presence of Thy glorious Mother and of all the Saints of the heavenly Court; that I want and desire, and it is my deliberate determination, if only it be Thy greater service and praise, to imitate Thee in bearing all injuries and all abuse and all poverty of spirit, and actual poverty, too, if Thy most Holy Majesty wants to choose and receive me to such life and state."[1]

THE SPIRITUAL EXERCISES

~ Since the story at the heart of this contemplation focuses on the search for the absent Jesus, it can speak powerfully to our own search for Jesus in our lives. We may find that we can very much relate to the mix of energies and emotions which Mary and Joseph might have experienced during this time—urgency, anxiety, fear, desire, relief, anger, and whatever other feelings your prayer might inspire, especially those that might mirror your own experiences of anxiety and fear at Jesus's absence at times in your life. This is also a passage which underscores the permissibility of letting your imagination push the boundaries of how you might typically understand things about the people and events described. Here we see that even scripture is not necessarily in accord with what we often take to be the case. Here it is not clear whether Joseph and Mary completely understand Jesus's importance or relationship to God, despite what might seem implications to the contrary in earlier passages. In light of such realities, we ought to feel a certain freedom to let God speak to us by means of our imagination in unexpected ways and not just according to our typical way of understanding these various mysteries.

☐ Of the Coming of Christ to the Temple When He Was of the Age of Twelve Years

First Point. First: Christ our Lord, of the age of twelve years, went up from Nazareth to Jerusalem.

Second Point. Second: Christ our Lord remained in Jerusalem, and His parents did not know it.

Third Point. Third: The three days passed, they found Him disputing in the Temple, and seated in the midst of the doctors, and His parents asking Him where He had been, He answered: "Did you not know that it behooves Me to be in the things which are My Father's?"

THE SPIRITUAL EXERCISES

1 When Ignatius speaks of "evangelical perfection" he is alluding to a life lived according to the "evangelical counsels," a term used to describe the radical commitment to religious life according to the traditional vows of poverty, chastity, and obedience. The distinction that Ignatius makes here between the first state and second state is reminiscent of Jesus's conversation with the rich young man. He is already living the first state, which is the observance of the commandments, having obeyed them since his youth. In response, Jesus invites him to the second state: "If you wish to be perfect, go, sell your possessions, and give the money to the poor, and you will have treasure in heaven; then come, follow me" (Matthew 19:21).

2 This meditation serves as a bridge between the contemplation of the early life of Jesus and our contemplation of various choices and states of life, culminating, if we are ready, in the election—our choice of the life to which Jesus has called us. The most basic expression of this life is found in these early contemplations on Jesus's life. The boy Jesus serves first as an example of the first state, being obedient to his parents and the other commandments. Then, leaving his parents to go to his Father's house, the temple, he anticipates the second state, leaving all behind—including his parents—to serve God.

3 Here is a basic movement of Ignatian prayer found repeatedly in the exercises. We are invited to consider and contemplate some episode in the life of Jesus, drawing what fruit we can from it. Then, the next step is to consider how, in a similar way, God is inviting us to imitate Jesus in the particular circumstances of our lives.

4 This passage serves as an introduction to Ignatius's "Meditation on the Two Standards," found in the second week of the exercises, in which we are asked to imagine first Satan, his attendants, and surroundings and how he might call us to follow him. Having done that, we are then invited to imagine the same for Jesus and to see him inviting us to follow him in his way. Though this is presented as a choice, Ignatius expects it to make clear that the only choice is to follow Jesus.

☐ The Obedience of Christ

The example which Christ our Lord, being under obedience to His parents, has given us for the first state,—which consists in the observance of the Commandments—having been now considered; and likewise for the second,—which is that of evangelical perfection,[1]—when He remained in the Temple, leaving His adoptive father and His natural Mother, to attend to the pure service of His eternal Father;[2] we will begin, at the same time contemplating His life, to investigate and to ask in what life or state His Divine Majesty wants to be served by us.[3] And so, for some introduction of it, we will, in the first Exercise following, see the intention of Christ our Lord, and, on the contrary, that of the enemy of human nature, and how we ought to dispose ourselves in order to come to perfection in whatever state of life God our Lord would give us to choose.[4]

The fact that this contemplation gives us the least to "go on" (only two verses from the gospel) should be seen as an opportunity rather than an obstacle. Of all the contemplations in *The Spiritual Exercises* this one, perhaps more than any other, allows us to explore fully the possibilities of how God can speak to us by means of our imagination. The fact that the scripture passage indicates that Jesus "advanced in wisdom, age, and grace," suggests to us that Jesus need not be understood or imagined as a superhuman child already blessed with all knowledge. Indeed, this contemplation can take us in various different directions, imagining at one time Jesus's more human attributes and experiences, another time his more divine. Given the possibilities, this is also a contemplation which is frequently prayed more than once. It also serves as something of a training ground, allowing the imagination to be more receptive to unexpected images and insights in later contemplations with more scriptural foundation.

Stories from the early life of Jesus provide a particularly rich opportunity for the use of imagination in prayer. Since we so often focus on and imagine Jesus as an older man engaged in public ministry, these contemplations allow us to see him with new eyes, coming to know him in a way we may not have previously imagined or thought important. Especially rich can be the contemplation here referred to as "Of the Life of Christ Our Lord from Twelve to Thirty Years," often referred to as Jesus's "hidden life," which relies completely on the imagination, since the gospels offer no recounting of Jesus's life during this period. Contemplating on how Jesus came to be who he was will not only deepen our relationship with Jesus but also help us to understand how we came to be who we are.

☐ Of the Life of Christ Our Lord from Twelve to Thirty Years

First Point. First: He was obedient to His parents: "He advanced in wisdom, age and grace."

Second Point. Second: It appears that He exercised the trade of carpenter, as St. Mark shows he means in the sixth chapter: "Perhaps this is that carpenter?"

THE SPIRITUAL EXERCISES

～ This episode marks the beginning of Jesus's public ministry at approximately the age of thirty years. The temptation here, especially given the voice from heaven described in the scriptural account, might be to begin to emphasize Jesus's divine nature in the subsequent meditations. However, as Ignatius emphasizes especially in the third week of contemplation on Jesus's suffering and death, we ought to, while recognizing Jesus's divinity, also imagine him as "hiding" his divinity so as to enter fully into the human experience. For in the first contemplation of the third week, Ignatius offers this observation: "The fifth, to consider how the Divinity hides Itself, that is, how It could destroy Its enemies and does not do it, and how It leaves the most sacred Humanity to suffer so very cruelly." To understand it this way does allow us in our contemplations to relate to Jesus not only as our Lord and Savior but also as a fellow human being. Indeed, this passage might even be seen to highlight this when Jesus insists that John baptize him, while not disputing the fact that from a "divine" perspective, it ought to be otherwise.

～ Jesus's temptation is another contemplation that might be varied not just according to one's imagination but also because the gospel accounts of the event are not identical. For example, it is only in Matthew's account, as Ignatius's third point describes, that angels come and minister to Jesus. In light of the comments on the previous contemplation, you can see how this might have some bearing on how the humanness of Jesus is perceived. It is also helpful to see here that primary among the things that Jesus is being tempted to do is assert his divine nature, which would undermine his mission. Jesus's temptation also highlights what Ignatius believed to be the three greatest temptations that we typically face—temptations to honor, riches, and power. This, like some of the other contemplations we have seen, is one that we would participate in primarily as an observer, though we might be moved to enter into a personal colloquy with Jesus after the temptation has finished.

☐ Of How Christ Was Baptized

First Point. First: Christ our Lord, after having taken leave of His Blessed Mother, came from Nazareth to the River Jordan, where St. John Baptist was.

Second Point. Second: St. John baptized Christ our Lord, and wanting to excuse himself, thinking himself unworthy of baptizing Him, Christ said to him: "Do this for the present, for so it is necessary that we fulfill all justice."

Third Point. Third: "The Holy Spirit came and the voice of the Father from heaven affirming: 'This is My beloved Son, in Whom I am well pleased.'"

THE SPIRITUAL EXERCISES

Of How Christ Was Tempted

First Point. First: After being baptized, He went to the Desert, where He fasted forty days and forty nights.

Second Point. Second: He was tempted by the enemy three times. "The tempter coming to Him said to Him: 'If Thou be the Son of God, say that these stones be turned into bread.' 'Cast Thyself down from here.' 'If prostrate on the earth Thou wilt adore me, I will give Thee all this which Thou seest.'"

Third Point. Third: "The Angels came and ministered to Him."

THE SPIRITUAL EXERCISES

1 One reason for the harassment of Ignatius and his early companions by the Inquisition was that they were suspected to be *alumbrados,* or "enlightened ones," a term referred to earlier and which described the members of a loosely organized quasi-mystical movement. Certainly one of the reasons that Ignatius was so concerned about the ideas and influence of Francisco Onfroy was that they shared some similarities with these heretical beliefs.

2 For the one committed to living spiritually, Ignatius assumes that there will be something of a symbiotic relationship between that life and the experience of persecution for the sake of Christ. Not only will we welcome insults and wrongs against us as a way of advancing in the spiritual life, but we will also desire such experiences as a means of experiencing solidarity with Jesus.

3 Ignatius developed a close relationship with the Portuguese royal family, who were great supporters of the Jesuits' work in that country. As this letter attests, Ignatius was eager to alleviate any concerns that King John might have about aligning himself with the work of the Jesuits. Ignatius wrote a letter of consolation to John when his only son and heir João died in 1554. João's widow, Princess Juana, also maintained close ties with Ignatius and the Jesuits, even later secretly being accepted into the Society of Jesus as a scholastic. Princess Juana holds the distinction of being the only female Jesuit in the history of the order.

☐ Desiring to Live Like Jesus

Should your highness wish to know why I was the object of all this scrutiny and investigation, you should know that it had nothing to do with schismatics, Lutherans, or *alumbrados*,[1] persons I never associated with or knew; the reason was surprise at an uneducated person like myself, particularly in Spain, speaking and conversing so extensively on spiritual subjects. And the truth is—our Lord, my creator and eternal judge, is my witness—that not for all the temporal power and riches under heaven would I wish that all this had not befallen me; indeed, I wish far worse would befall me, to the greater glory of his Divine Majesty ... For the greater a desire we attain (barring offense on the part of our neighbor) of being clothed in the livery of Christ our Lord, namely, insults, false witness, and every other kind of wrongs, the more we will advance in spirit and win spiritual riches, with which, if we are living spiritually, our soul longs to be wholly adorned."[2]

LETTER TO KING JOHN III OF PORTUGAL[3]

1 The first stage of humility is similar to the first state of life that Igna-tius has us consider after these meditations on Jesus's early life. It is a commitment to living according to the Ten Commandments, obeying God and God's law. While clearly Ignatius's hope is that we would live a life "above and beyond" these simple expectations, he does grant that only this first humility is "necessary for salvation."

2 The second stage of humility is for us to desire and accept whatever type of life that comes as a consequence of our service of God whether that means being rich or poor, living a long or short life, and so on.

3 The third stage of humility is the most radical. It involves not just accepting but *desiring* that we experience poverty, persecution, and loss of prestige so as to more authentically live as Jesus lived. This underscores the extent to which the radical imitation of Christ we encountered in the "Kingdom Prayer" is an ideal for Ignatius. How-ever, the "Three Kinds of Humility" also demonstrate the extent to which Ignatius tries to reconcile the ideal and the real. Note that only the first humility is "necessary for salvation," despite Ignatius's obvi-ous belief that God is better served in the more radical second and third kinds of humility. It is in the nature of Ignatius's practical mysti-cism always to present the ideal as something to strive for while simul-taneously making allowances for the fact that many will not be prepared for, or even called to achieve, the ideal.

☐ The Humility of Christ

The Three Kinds of Humility

First Humility. The first manner of Humility is necessary for eternal salvation; namely, that I so lower and so humble myself, as much as is possible to me, that in everything I obey the law of God, so that, even if they made me lord of all the created things in this world, nor for my own temporal life, I would not be in deliberation about breaking a Commandment, whether Divine or human, which binds me under mortal sin.[1]

Second Humility. The second is more perfect Humility than the first; namely, if I find myself at such a stage that I do not want, and feel no inclination to have, riches rather than poverty, to want honor rather than dishonor, to desire a long rather than a short life—the service of God our Lord and the salvation of my soul being equal; and so not for all creation, nor because they would take away my life, would I be in deliberation about committing a venial sin.[2]

Third Humility. The third is most perfect Humility; namely, when—including the first and second, and the praise and glory of the Divine Majesty being equal—in order to imitate and be more actually like Christ our Lord, I want and choose poverty with Christ poor rather than riches, opprobrium with Christ replete with it rather than honors; and to desire to be rated as worthless and a fool for Christ, Who first was held as such, rather than wise or prudent in this world.[3]

THE SPIRITUAL EXERCISES

1 As concerned as Ignatius is with encouraging us to avoid vanity, or thinking more of ourselves than is merited, he sees an even greater danger in adopting a "wrong humility," a state in which we think so little of ourselves that we fail to share the gifts that we have received from God. From Ignatius's perspective, vanity might even be seen as the lesser error, as those of us inclined to boast of our achievements would be more likely to share our gifts rather than squander them.

2 Another help in resisting the temptation to vanity is to see how God is making good use of others and their talents, often in ways that seem superior to us, or in ways that might make us envious because we are incapable of doing the same. It is a spur to humility, and also helps make us more aware that our gifts are not necessarily any better or worse than another's gifts, but simply different.

☐ Pride and False Humility

Next, the enemy resorts to his second weapon; that is to say, pride and vainglory. He intimates to the person that he possesses much goodness and holiness, placing him higher than he deserves. If the servant of God resists these arrows by humbling and abasing himself and refusing to consent to the enemy's suggestions, he comes with his third weapon, a wrong humility.[1] Seeing how good and humble the Lord's servant is, how while fulfilling what the Lord commands, he still considers it useless, looks only to his own weakness, not to any vainglory, he gives the person the thought that if he discovers anything that God our Lord has given him by way either of deeds or of resolves and desires, he sins through another species of vainglory by speaking in his own favor. He thus tries to keep the person from talking about the good things he has received from his Lord, so that he will not produce fruit in others or in himself. For to recall what one has already received is always a help toward even greater things—although this speaking must be with great moderation and only for people's greater benefit, that is, one's own or that of other persons one sees are properly disposed and likely to believe the speaker and be benefited. Thus, by getting us to be humble, the enemy manages to draw us on to a wrong humility, namely, to one that is excessive and flawed.

LETTER TO TERESA REJADELL

When those who think they are doing a great deal see the work of others and [note] how God is making use of them, they have cause to humble themselves and acknowledge their own lukewarmness.[2]

LETTER TO THE ENTIRE SOCIETY

1 Given the similar trajectory of their two lives, Ignatius may well have seen a kindred spirit in Francis of Assisi. Both came from prominent families, served as soldiers, and had a conversion experience that followed upon their experience of battle—Francis while as a prisoner of war, and Ignatius during his convalescence from battle injuries. Eventually, Ignatius, like Francis, would forsake his former life by trading his clothing with a beggar. Like Francis, Ignatius became convinced that God was calling him to a far off land to help convert the Muslims there. In both cases, their attempts to follow that path proved a failure, failures that eventually led to the founding of their respective religious orders. This is not to overlook their differences, of course. While both men benefited from mystical experiences, Francis lacked Ignatius's more practical approach and his skill as a master organizer, yet both were responsible for significant innovations in the religious life of their time.

2 This is a recounting of the initial stages of Ignatius's conversion when, to his great surprise, he discovered a strong desire to become a saint in the mold of those who had come before him. Interestingly, the two saints he mentions by name, Francis and Dominic, were both founders of newer, non-monastic religious orders whose members, unlike monks, were less tied to a specific house or geographical location.While their prayer practices were similar to monastic communities, they also spent a significant amount of time away from their communities, doing public ministry and engaging in missionary work. Ignatius's Society of Jesus was most certainly inspired by these other orders, while departing even further from the monastic model, shedding a regular schedule of mandatory communal prayer and emphasizing availability for mission over stable attachment to a geographical community.

☐ Imitating the Saints

Nevertheless Our Lord assisted him, causing other thoughts, that arouse from the things he read, to follow these. For in reading the life of Our Lord and of the saints, he stopped to think, reasoning within himself, "What if I should do this which St. Francis[1] did, and this which St. Dominic did?" Thus he pondered over many things that he found good, always proposing to himself what was difficult and burdensome and as he so proposed, it seemed easy for him to accomplish it. But he did not more than argue with himself, saying, "St. Dominic did this, so I have to do it; St. Francis did this, so I have to do it."[2]

MEMOIRS, 8

1 In this meditation Ignatius highlights the fact that our calling to follow Jesus can have multiple dimensions, or stages, as it evolves from a temporary to a deeper and more permanent commitment. This awareness is important for us in order to be patient with ourselves—and others—as we all advance at a different pace in the Christian life.

2 This meditation serves to help one reflect on one's own calling. Because of the way it is expressed, the meditation helps to remedy certain assumptions anyone who is undertaking the Ignatian exercises might have about him- or herself. Persons of wealth and privilege, by reflecting on the "low condition" of the earliest apostles, are challenged to give up the idea that their status makes them especially worthy of God's call. By the same token, this meditation is also helpful to those who because of their poverty or sense of unworthiness might think themselves incapable of a special calling from God.

☐ Following the Call of the Apostles

First Point. First: it seems that St. Peter and St. Andrew were called three times: first, to some knowledge; this is clear from St. John in the first Chapter: secondly, to follow Christ in some way with the purpose of returning to possess what they had left, as St. Luke says in the fifth Chapter: thirdly, to follow Christ our Lord forever, as St. Matthew says in the fourth Chapter and St. Mark in the first.[1]

Second Point. Second: He called Philip, as is in the first Chapter of St. John, and Matthew as Matthew himself says in the ninth Chapter.

Third Point. Third: He called the other Apostles, of whose special call the Gospel does not make mention.

And three other things also would be to be considered:

The first, how the Apostles were of uneducated and low condition;

The second, the dignity to which they were so sweetly called;

The third, the gifts and graces by which they were raised above all the Fathers of the New and Old Testaments.[2]

THE SPIRITUAL EXERCISES

1 "He" in this case is Francisco Onfroy, mentioned earlier. Onfroy tried to convince Francis Borgia and other Jesuits that authentic religious life required constant, unceasing prayer which was the hallmark of the contemplative orders such as the Benedictines. Jesuits, by contrast, were meant by Ignatius to be "contemplatives in action," living a less structured life that was focused on mission, while also maintaining a regular prayer life.

2 Lest we think that Ignatius was simply averse to lengthy prayer, it is important to note that the alternative vocation to religious life that he had taken most seriously was becoming a Carthusian monk. The Carthusians are among the strictest monastic orders and spend the majority of their time in silent work and prayer. Indeed, Ignatius always believed there to be a special kinship between Jesuits and Carthusians. He assumed that the most natural transition for a Jesuit who sought a life more devoted to prayer would be to join them. In the spirit of this letter, however, he would be quick to point out that not even the Carthusians practiced the life of constant, lengthy prayer of the sort that Onfroy proposed.

3 Ultimately, Ignatius's point is that most of the saints, and even Jesus himself, approached prayer far more practically, balancing it out with good works, spending time with others, studying, preaching, and writing. As important as prayer is, one might imagine Ignatius saying, it alone cannot make a saint.

☐ Praying Like Jesus and the Saints

First, consider the example of Christ: although he sometimes spent the night in prayer, at other times he did not spend so much, as in his prayer at the supper or his three prayers in the garden ... He[1] would do well to reflect that it is not only in prayer that God makes us of a person; otherwise, anything less than twenty-four hours of prayer a day, if such a thing were possible, would be too short, since every person should give himself to God as totally as possible. But the fact is that there are times when God is served more by other things than by prayer, so much so that for their sake God is happy that prayer be relinquished—and all the more that it be shortened.[2] Thus, we should indeed "pray always and faint not," but we should understand this rightly, as the saints and doctors understand it.[3]

LETTER TO FRANCIS BORGIA

1 Ignatius repeatedly warns of the dangerous temptations of riches, honor, and pride. Even if it is unlikely that one would attain a perfect state of poverty, worldly indifference to the point of suffering insult and injury (that is what he means by "contempt"), and humility, Ignatius believed that striving for these things would lead at the very least to an increase in virtue.

2 Though for Ignatius, as in the third humility, this is the ideal, he still insists that we examine ourselves, our motivations, and our actions, so that we don't sin or displease God by overdoing it, or risking harm to ourselves or others.

☐ Poverty

Third Point. The third, to consider the discourse which Christ our Lord makes to all His servants and friends whom He sends on this expedition, recommending them to want to help all, by bringing them first to the highest spiritual poverty, and—if His Divine Majesty would be served and would want to choose them—no less to actual poverty; the second is to be of contumely and contempt; because from these two things humility follows. So that there are to be three steps; the first, poverty against riches; the second, contumely or contempt against worldly honor; the third, humility against pride. And from these three steps let them induce to all the other virtues.[1]

First Colloquy. One Colloquy to Our Lady, that she may get me grace from Her Son and Lord that I may be received under His standard; and first in the highest spiritual poverty, and—if His Divine Majesty would be served and would want to choose and receive me—not less in actual poverty; second, in suffering contumely and injuries, to imitate Him more in them, if only I can suffer them without the sin of any person, or displeasure of His Divine Majesty.[2]

The Spiritual Exercises

1 By "holy poverty," Ignatius means *voluntary poverty*, chosen for the service of God, rather than poverty that comes upon us through misfortune or through our own fault.

2 "Poverty of spirit" may or may not be accompanied by material poverty. It refers more to a state of mind, or a way of approaching the world. When we possess "poverty of spirit," it means that we are indifferent to the possession and accumulation of material things, but it can still mean that we possess those things that we need, and thus are not *actually* poor. So we can be spiritually poor without being materially poor. However, poverty of spirit makes it more likely that we will strive to be materially poor as well, according to what God wills for us.

3 Ignatius celebrates the freedom that comes with poverty voluntarily undertaken—freeing us from some worldly cares, making us more dependent upon and responsive to God, and contributing to the development of other virtues.

4 Because the Jesuit college in Padua was not receiving sufficient support from its founder and principal benefactor, the Jesuits there were lacking in many of the basic things that most Jesuit communities would have. This letter was written, then, to encourage Jesuits who were enduring actual poverty above and beyond their holy poverty.

☐ The Blessings of Poverty

But if we look to genuine advantages inherent in the means that are suited to help us attain our final end, we will see that holy poverty[1] keeps us from many sins by removing the occasions for them, for "poverty lacks the wherewithal to feed its love." Poverty crushes the worm of the rich, pride; it cuts off the hellish leeches of lust and gluttony, and many other sins as well. And if through weakness a person falls, poverty helps him to rise at once. For it is free of that love which, like birdlime, binds the heart to earth and to earthly things and takes away our ability to rise up again and turn back to God. Poverty enables us in every circumstance to hear the voice (that is, the inspiration) of the Holy Spirit better, because it removes the obstructions that keep it out. It makes our prayers more powerful with God, for "the Lord has heard the prayer of the poor" [Psalm 10:17]. It lets us go forward unimpeded on the path of virtue, like travelers freed from all burdens. It frees us from the slavery common to so many of the great ones of the world, where "everything obeys or serves money" [see Ecclesiastes 10:19]. When it is poverty of spirit,[2] it lets the soul be filled with every virtue, for the emptier the soul is of love for earthly things, the fuller it will be of God through his gifts.... Thus, those who voluntarily make themselves poor in human possessions will necessarily be rich in the gifts of God.[3]

LETTER TO THE MEMBERS OF THE SOCIETY IN PADUA[4]

1 Throughout Ignatius's life and beyond, many in the church continued to criticize Ignatius's choice of "The Society of Jesus" as the name of his religious community. It was thought to be presumptuous; so much so that more than once in the early history of the Jesuits some members of the hierarchy unsuccessfully tried to have the name changed.

2 As these questions suggest, the poverty practiced by the Jesuits was not destitution. Though it required simple living, it did not mean being poor in appearance, in diet, or resulting in poor health. The poverty of Jesuits was not meant to be so extreme that it interfered with their ability to serve God as they should. For example, many early Jesuits held positions in royal courts, and they could not appear for work looking disheveled or homeless.

3 Ignatius shows by these imagined conversations his belief that the tradition of begging alms, practiced by many religious orders such as the Franciscans, not only helped support the community financially, but also exposed those doing the begging to real experiences of poverty, contempt, and humility.

☐ Begging Alms

The formula for asking alms is, "Give alms to the Society of Jesus for the love of God."

1. When people scoff about the Society's name, the answer is, "This was the name that was given to our order by the supreme pontiffs."**1**

2. When people reproach them for being fat, they should answer, "Even fat people need to eat; they have a human constitution."

3. When people say, "You are hale and hardy," answer: "I want to spend my strength and hardiness well in God's service."

4. When people say, "You are well clothed," answer: "If we were rich, we would not be begging alms."**2**

5. When persons of importance ask, "Why do you go begging alms?" answer, "Because need obliges us to, and in order to imitate our fathers, who also did this."

The more usual response will be, "Brother, give us alms for the love of God."**3**

INSTRUCTION: "HOW TO ASK FOR ALMS"

Part 8
Union of Mind and Heart

1 What Ignatius speaks of here is reflected in the training process for Jesuits both then and now. Jesuit training involves two major periods of study interrupted by a period of full-time work in ministry, usually lasting two to three years. This is, in part, a way of ensuring that the Jesuit is capable of devoting sufficient energy to both ministry and studies. As Ignatius implies here, it is possible that he might succeed in studies but fail to apply the same energy to other work.

2 All the excerpts in this section are drawn from the same letter that Ignatius wrote to the scholastics and fathers at Coimbra. As the excerpts included here reveal, he was attempting to address an imbalance that was becoming problematic in the Portuguese province. The province was blessed with many enthusiastic Jesuits in training, but there were concerns that the Jesuit superior there was not encouraging sufficient moderation on the part of his sometimes overzealous subjects. Because the letter is so comprehensive, it gives both a fascinating glimpse of the early Jesuits and offers deep insights on a host of topics. Among Ignatius's letters, this one is sufficiently rich to reward multiple readings and reflections.

3 By saying that lukewarmness makes us "undeserving of God's help," Ignatius underscores how dangerous he believes it to be. It perpetuates a focus on the self rather than on God, depriving us of the peace found when focusing our energies on God, and placing them at God's disposal.

4 Ignatius also wants to warn us against the mistaken notion that holy fervor in this life has consequences only for the next life. It also has an effect on our general disposition and our ability to trust in God's help in our lives and ministry now.

☐ Holy Ardor and Growth in Virtue

And so for the love of God do not be slack or tepid. For, as they say, if tautness breaks the bow, idleness breaks the soul; whereas Solomon says that "the soul of those who work shall become fat." Try to maintain holy and discerning ardor in working to acquire both learning and virtues. In either of these, a single intense act is worth a thousand listless ones; an energetic person achieves in a short time what a lazy one fails to attain in many years.

In studies there is a clear difference between the hard-working and the negligent, but the same is true in overcoming the passions and weaknesses to which our nature is subject, and in acquiring the virtues.[1] It is certain that the listless, by not struggling against themselves, only late in life or even never attain peace of soul or the full possession of any virtue, whereas the energetic and hard-working make great strides in both areas.

LETTER TO THE FATHERS AND SCHOLASTICS AT COIMBRA[2]

Don't Be Lukewarm

Luke-warmness ... keeps a person living in constant anxieties, for it prevents him from getting rid of their cause—self-love—and makes us undeserving of God's help.[3] So you should summon up great courage to work hard at your praiseworthy exercises; for even in this life you will experience the value of holy fervor, not only in the perfecting of your souls but also in your peace of mind during this present life.[4]

LETTER TO THE FATHERS AND SCHOLASTICS AT COIMBRA

1 Jesuit training has always been a lengthy process, and we see something of Ignatius's rationale for that here. The early Jesuits tended to be men of great energy who might be apt to charge into difficult situations insufficiently prepared, or to blindly make imprudent choices. The lengthy training process both helped to weed out the insufficiently committed and helped teach the committed the patience that would help them to guard against over-commitment and rashness.

2 Here we have a classic image going back at least to the sixth century. That is when Saint John Climacus (so named because of this work) wrote the ascetical classic *The Ladder of Divine Ascent*, in which each rung of the ladder represents a different virtue. This image of the ladder appeared in subsequent centuries, including a famous icon depicting Saint John at the top of the ladder, which can be found at St. Catherine's Monastery on Mt. Sinai. An inclined ladder is depicted, with monks at various stages of the ladder, some of whom are trying to be pulled down by demon-like figures. It is clear, as Ignatius states, that the higher one ascends the ladder, the more dangerous the fall becomes. Sin does not just cause one to falter but to fall off or back to the bottom of the ladder. Ignatius was clearly acquainted with this idea and may very well have read Saint John Climacus's treatise at some point in his studies or in his spiritual reading.

3 "He" refers to Ignatius, as this is a letter he commissioned but did not write himself.

4 This is the spirit by which, as mentioned earlier, we might come to understand our studies or work as acts of devotion.

☐ The Need for Balance

What I have said so far in order to arouse the sleeping and spur on those who linger and loiter on the way should not be taken as occasion for going to the opposite extreme of indiscreet fervor.[1] "Yours should be a rational service," said St. Paul [Romans 12:1], for he knew the truth of the Psalmist's words, "The king's honor loves judgment," [Psalm 99:4], that is, discretion ... Thus, as St. Bernard says, the enemy has no more effective device for robbing a person of genuine charity of heart than by getting him to proceed therein heedlessly and without spiritual reasonableness.... Without this moderation, good turns into evil and virtue into vice; and numerous bad consequences ensue, contrary to the intentions of the one proceeding this way.... Gains made too hastily in this way usually do not last ... the higher he was, the more dangerously will he fall—not halting until he comes to the bottom of the ladder.[2]

LETTER TO THE FATHERS AND SCHOLASTICS AT COIMBRA

No Need For Excessive Prayer

As to prayer and meditation, except where there is a special need because of bothersome or dangerous temptations, as I said earlier, I notice that he[3] approves endeavoring to find God in everything one does rather than spending long blocks of time on prayer. This is the spirit he desires to see in members of the Society;[4] that, if possible, they should find no less devotion in any work of charity or obedience than in prayer or meditation. For they should not be doing anything at all except for the love and service of God our Lord, and each one

(continued on page 235)

5 This is the peace and confidence that comes with turning our lives and will over to God, so that all we do is for God's glory, especially those things—in the case of the Jesuits—which are commanded by our religious superiors.

6 Ignatius is not advocating a philosophy sometimes expressed by religious professionals, "my work is my prayer," nor is he encouraging excessive prayer like Onfroy. Rather, he is emphasizing an awareness that there are frequent opportunities to find God in what we do and experience, and that this, in turn, is a way of reminding ourselves of our commitment to God.

7 Urbano Fernandes was appointed superior over the scholastics studying in Coimbra in 1551. In this letter, Ignatius answers some of his questions about the job and offers him some advice about how to care for and govern the scholastics.

should find greater satisfaction in doing what he is commanded,[5] because he can then have no doubt that he is conforming himself to do the will of God our Lord.[6]

LETTER TO URBANO FERNANDES[7]

⟨∾⟩ Though there are various motivations for the advice that Ignatius gives about preaching here, given the historical context, much of what he says is just good general advice for any of us who are asked to preach or to speak on theological topics. He urges Jesuit preachers to be attentive to their responsibilities not only to educate, but to be sensitive to their hearers' needs and capacities, and to strive to move them to acts of charity, devotion, and a desire to live virtuously.

1 Though a major concern of the Council of Trent was precisely to address "points where Protestants differ from Catholics," Ignatius urges them not to make this part of their work and preaching outside of the council. Instead, he encourages them to do what he thought more important: moving them toward religious devotion, virtue, and the love of God. Undoubtedly, Ignatius probably assumed this would have the effect of also moving some away from the attractions of Protestantism. He would have known that the council would be likely to address some of these issues directly (as it did), and that the more positively directed preaching of the Jesuits would help the people of Trent to be inclined to receiving the pronouncements of the council more positively.

2 In 1546, at the request of Pope Paul III, Ignatius sent Diego Lainez, Alfonso Salmerón, Claude Jay, and Pierre Favre to be theological advisors to the council. Favre died as he was making his way to the council and so never fulfilled this mission. As the council progressed, the Jesuit Peter Canisius, who would become famous for his work in Germany, also joined the others in their work at the council. Lainez's experience at Trent would have served him well when, after Ignatius's death in 1556, he succeeded Ignatius as father general of the Jesuits.

☐ Preaching

In preaching, I would not touch upon any points where Protestants differ from Catholics; I would merely exhort to virtuous living and to the Church's devotions, urging souls to thorough self-knowledge and to greater knowledge and love of their creator and Lord. I would frequently mention the council and, as indicated above, conclude each sermon with a prayer for it.[1]

LETTER TO THE FATHERS OF THE COUNCIL OF TRENT[2]

3 The scholastic approach to theology emphasized human reason and sought to bring together philosophy and theology. It was the standard method for doing theology throughout the Middle Ages, though other approaches began to challenge the scholastic—most prominent among them humanistic philosophy—in the fifteenth and sixteenth centuries. Its preeminent philosopher and theologian was Thomas Aquinas, whose *Summa Theologica* is perhaps the greatest example of this approach to theology. During the time of Ignatius, moreover, there was a renewed emphasis on scholasticism in the theological training of Jesuit clergy, partly in reaction to the emergence of Protestantism.

4 In a roundabout way, Ignatius seems to be encouraging these preachers to be sensitive to their audience, adjusting the level of their preaching to their audience's needs and capacities. This was another advantage of the Jesuit commitment to the teaching of children, for this experience made them better equipped to adapt their message to their audience.

5 Given the Jesuit emphasis on studies and the contentious atmosphere between Catholics and Protestants in Germany at the time, the temptation for many Jesuits would have been to rely on their academic training. Ignatius knew, however, that simple academic disputation would not be enough to change people's hearts, who needed both inspiration and motivation to love God and to desire a holy life.

6 As in *The Spiritual Exercises*, Ignatius would have viewed the use of scripture in preaching and lectures as more of a spiritual exercise than a scholarly one. Lectures on the Bible would be more inclined toward encouraging the imitation of Jesus, the apostles, and other holy figures.

7 Despite the fact that Ignatius's advice tends to avoid discussion of Protestant and Catholic differences, he takes it for granted that Jesuits being sent to Germany (one of the centers of the Protestant movement) would be engaged in such discussion and disputes whether they liked it or not. Thus, although he doesn't say it outright, his advice for preaching would certainly focus on whatever would encourage the faithful to be more open to Catholic belief and doctrine.

1. The first thing is to do well in your public lectures; these are the main thing for which you were requested by the duke and sent by the Sovereign Pontiff. You should give solid doctrine without too much Scholastic terminology,[3] which tends to put people off, particularly when abstruse: the lectures should be learned but comprehensible. They should be regular but not too long or too rhetorical. Prudence will dictate how much use to make of disputations and other academic exercises.[4]

2. To increase your audience and be of most benefit to them, you should not only nourish the mind but also add things that will nourish the religious affections, so that hearers go home from your lectures not just more learned but better persons.[5]

3. In addition to the Scholastic lectures, it would be good to have sermons or biblical lectures on feast days. The aim of these is less to instruct the intellect than to move the affections and shape behavior.[6]

LETTER TO JESUITS LEAVING FOR GERMANY[7]

1 Ignatius repeatedly made this and similar points to Jesuits in the midst of their studies. Knowing their apostolic zeal, he was quite aware that many (as he did himself) would find studies tedious in comparison to the ministry in which they could already be engaged. His main point is that the pursuit of God's will by means of study, no matter how tedious or futile it might seem at times, serves God's purposes in ways that we cannot always know. Ignatius knew that they would see the benefit of their hard work and patience when they undertook their future ministries.

2 This advice is helpful for anyone engaged in preparation for a future career or ministry—training that, for the present, may limit our opportunities to be more actively involved in the work to which we have been called. Ignatius insists that however mundane or distracting from one's true desires this might seem, it is also serving God.

3 Jesuit scholastics, mentioned throughout, are technically those Jesuits who have not yet professed their final vows. This refers largely to Jesuits who are in studies prior to their ordination as priests and more often than not specifically to this group. However, Jesuit priests who have not yet professed their final vows, but are no longer in studies, are still technically considered scholastics as well.

4 At times it may seem that Ignatius claims that prayer is secondary to study, or perhaps not even necessary. It is important to read such statements in the context of these "exercises for growth in virtue," which, Ignatius assumes, the Jesuits he is addressing are already practicing on a daily basis, even during the time of studies.

5 An alternative approach to the daily self-examination is to examine one's day with attention to identifying those moments associated with particular areas of concern in our lives. So, for example, if we have a tendency to be more short-tempered than usual, we might examine our day with an eye to identifying those moments when we lost our temper, meditating and praying about why this was this case, and asking God's help in this area.

☐ Studies

And do not imagine that during the interval of studies you are not being useful to your neighbor.[1] Over and above the advantage to yourself (which is demanded by well-ordered charity: "Have pity on your own soul, fearing God," [Sirach 30:14] you are serving God's honor and glory in many ways.[2]

LETTER TO THE FATHERS AND SCHOLASTICS AT COIMBRA

Finding God through Studies

In the view of the end of our studies, the scholastics[3] cannot engage in long meditations. Over and above the exercises for growth in virtue (daily Mass, an hour for vocal prayer and the examen of conscience, weekly confession and Communion),[4] they can practice seeking the presence of our Lord in all things: in their dealings with other people, their walking, seeing, tasting, hearing, understanding, and all our activities. For his Divine Majesty truly is in everything by his presence, power, and essence. This kind of meditation—finding God our Lord in everything—is easier than lifting ourselves up and laboriously making ourselves present to more abstracted divine realities. Moreover, by making us properly disposed, this excellent exercise will bring great visitations of our Lord even in short prayer. In addition, one can practice frequently offering to God our Lord his studies along with the effort that these demand, keeping in mind that we undertake them for his love and setting aside our personal tastes so as to render some service to his Divine Majesty by helping those for whose life he died. We could also make these two practices the matter of our examen.[5]

LETTER TO ANTONIO BRANDÃO

241

⟨∼⟩ This is a useful reminder of how often we are tempted not by evil, but by good and worthwhile things that draw us away from what we ought to be doing. This requires frequent discernment. There are any number of good and holy activities in which we could be engaged, but they would tempt us away from what God intends us to be doing right now.

1 Here Ignatius expands on the previous insight. During Ignatius's own period of studies, he determined that in some ways it was necessary for studies to be dry and tedious, for he found that intense experiences of spiritual consolation, which he might have expected to be an aid to his work, actually proved a hindrance. Interestingly, he discovered that even something that under most circumstances would be a grace, could in certain instances, like during a period of studies, be recognized instead as a temptation.

⟨∼⟩ In his own way, Ignatius challenges us to reconsider what we understand as religious devotion or devotional practices. Devotion can take on unusual and surprising forms when we undertake even the most menial tasks as part of our service of God. Cleaning a basement might become as devotional an act as lighting a candle; driving our child to school might involve more religious devotion than marching in a religious procession.

2 The previous insight also highlights an alternative temptation, suggested here. Many students would experience not intense spiritual consolation but rather intense spiritual dryness. This could lead some to despair that they had somehow lost touch with God, who had inspired their vocation. Ignatius reminds them that the very fact that their studies are done in God's service should be enough to allay such fears.

3 Bartolomeo Hernandez was community superior for the Jesuits at the Jesuit college in Salamanca, a community made up mostly of scholastics who were engaged in studies as well as in various forms of ministry. Ignatius was writing to reassure Hernandez that a lack of deliberate religious devotion among the scholastics in studies was not something to be concerned about.

☐ Spiritual Temptations

So, returning to Barcelona, he began to study with great diligence. But one thing was very much in his way: that is, when he began to memorize, as one must in the beginnings of grammar, there came to him new insights into spiritual matters and fresh relish, to such an extent that he could not memorize, nor could he drive them away no matter how much he resisted.

So, thinking about this, he said to himself, "Not even when I engage in prayer and am at Mass do such vivid insights come to me." Thus, little by little, he came to realize it was a temptation.[1]

MEMOIRS, 79

It is no cause for wonder that not all of our own students experience the relish of devotion that one might desire. He who dispenses this grace does so where and when he thinks fit. During the time of studies, which impose considerable spiritual effort, we may presume that divine Wisdom sometimes suspends sensible visitations of this sort, for although they give great delight to the spirit, they sometimes excessively weaken the body. Moreover, the occupation of the mind with academic pursuits naturally tends to produce a certain dryness in the interior affections. However, when the study is directed purely to God's service, it is an excellent form of devotion.[2]

LETTER TO BARTOLOMEO HERNANDEZ[3]

~ Ignatius required frequent letters and reports from Jesuit superiors. As he suggests here, he believed the responsibility to report on what a single Jesuit or group of Jesuits was doing helped to guarantee the quality of the work and provided a greater awareness overall about what God was accomplishing through them. In our individual spiritual lives, Ignatius's principle can be applied in the ways in which we hold ourselves accountable, whether it means keeping a regular journal or meeting regularly with a spiritual director for conversation and advice.

1 Throughout its history the Society of Jesus has been accused at times of being overly secretive, and sometimes this complaint is justifiable. Yet, here we see the good intentions out of which such secrecy may result. Not all things that might be recorded by the community, such as certain internal disciplinary matters, are necessary or even prudent to make public.

2 Anyone who has regretted writing an angry or overly emotional letter in haste, with little thought to the consequences, or thought to how it might be received or interpreted, will understand what Ignatius means here.

~ At a time in history when so much of what we say or write lacks privacy and/or can be recorded permanently, this advice Ignatius offers for his own time can be very helpfully applied to our current circumstances. In a time of instant communication, the kind of prudence in composition that he suggests could easily be overlooked. Yet, the care that he advises the letter writer to take ought to even be more carefully and deliberately observed by writers of e-mails, blogs, and tweets.

3 Ignatius met Pierre Favre at the University of Paris, and Favre was one of his closest and most devoted companions. He was among the group of first companions who founded the Society of Jesus, and the first to be ordained a priest. As noted above, he had been chosen to be a theological advisor at the Council of Trent, but died before he could get there. This letter to Favre about writing about Jesuit activities was also sent to Jesuits reporting back to Rome from various places around the world.

□ Writing

Having to report about what one is doing from day to day can serve as a stimulus for being more alert to doing something that can be written about.

LETTER TO THE ENTIRE SOCIETY

Advice for Writers

I will describe what I myself do, and I trust in the Lord, will continue to do in this regard so as to avoid mistakes when writing to members of the Society. I make a first draft of the main letter, reporting things that will be edifying; then, after reading it over and correcting it, keeping in mind that it is going to be read by everybody, I write or have someone write it out a second time. For we must give even more thought to what we write than to what we say. Writing is permanent and gives lasting witness; we cannot mend or reinterpret it as easily as we can our speech. And even with all this I am sure I make many mistakes, and fear doing so in the future. I leave for the separate pages other details that are inappropriate for the main letter or lacking in edification.[1] These pages each one can write hastily "out of the overflow of the heart,"[2] with or without careful organization.

LETTER TO PIERRE FAVRE[3]

4 This offers a good sense of how Ignatius understood humility. We should not fear writing about what we are accomplishing with the help of God. However, we should do so while also recognizing our faults, and with concern for the edification of others. And, if we feel we need to guard against vanity, we can take Ignatius's advice and let others report our extraordinary deeds, rather than doing so ourselves.

∿ Today many of us receive multiple messages each day, which we are not always able to respond to right away. Here Ignatius offers some good advice for dealing swiftly, and with the proper attention and focus, to the most important items among them. Many of us have learned the advantage of taking the time to answer something right away, even if we don't always manage to do it.

Write As If Everybody Will Read It

A person writing about his own labors and what God is working in souls should, while telling all the facts, remember to write as if everybody were going to see his letter; he should express himself in such a manner that the reader will see that he is seeking to further not his own but God's glory and the edification of the neighbor, and to obey by writing what is commanded, attributing wholly to God what is God's, that is, all that is good, and to himself what is his own, namely, all that is evil, etc. If there is something so extraordinarily laudable that he does not wish to report it in his own words, it would be good if he had a friend who could write about it; if not, it should come on a separate sheet, or else in the main letter in such a way that even somewhat suspicious persons would have no room for suspecting him of vanity.[4]

LETTER TO THE ENTIRE SOCIETY

A Fresh and Careful Reply

If some point in the letter requires careful response or some commission is given to you, this may be specially noted; and if it might quickly slip from your attention, it would be good to do the thing or give what reply you can while the matter is fresh in your mind, even if the letter should remain in your room until you send it or until a fuller response occurs to you.

LETTER TO THE ENTIRE SOCIETY

1 Antonio Araoz was the nephew of Ignatius's sister-in-law. Antonio became a Jesuit and was later named the first provincial of Spain. Like many of Ignatius's correspondents, Araoz had to be warned against overwork on a number of occasions. As many new Jesuit colleges were about to be established in Spain, Ignatius shared with Araoz his reflections on Jesuit education, based on his experience of the Jesuit colleges in Italy.

2 From the beginning to the present this has been a key element of the Jesuit approach to education. The goal was not only to teach, but also, as the motto of many Jesuit high schools today claims, to form "men and women for others." Jesuit education has always sought to instill in its students knowledge, talents, and virtues that would allow them to be a force for the betterment of both society and the church.

☐ The Value of Teaching

Those who teach make progress themselves and learn a great deal by teaching others, acquiring greater confidence and mastery in their learning.

LETTER TO ANTONIO ARAOZ[1]

From among those who are at present only students, various persons will in time emerge—some for preaching and the care of souls, others for the government of the land and the administration of justice, and others for other responsibilities. In short, since young people turn into adults, their good formation in life and learning will benefit many others, with the fruit expanding more widely every day.[2]

LETTER TO ANTONIO ARAOZ

3 Many would find what Ignatius states as these Jesuits' "main purpose" surprising, since they were being sent to be theological advisors to a church council. Yet, this shows what Ignatius's image of what a Jesuit's (and indeed any Christian's) main purpose was. As is clear from this passage, Ignatius believed that there is a direct relationship between the amount of time we spend doing these basic corporal works of mercy and our success in other Christian endeavors. Thus, the theologians' time spent preaching, hearing confessions, visiting the poor and sick, and so on would only increase the likelihood of their success in their work for the council. Prominent among these tasks for the Jesuits would be the teaching of children, a task which has always been thought one of the Jesuit's most important works. Ignatius thought it so important, in fact, that a Jesuit professing final vows makes an additional promise to be engaged in the teaching of children.

4 "Divine Providence" refers to the work of God to bring things about in unseen ways. When something unexpected happens with a good result, we often refer to such happenings as "providential." Though we acknowledge that divine grace can influence or affect an outcome, it does not mean that we are meant to simply await the work of providence. If that were all there was to the spiritual life, discernment would not be necessary. An approach to the spiritual life based solely on the whims of providence—"If it happens, God wills it; if it doesn't happen, God doesn't will it"—is precisely the kind of approach that Ignatius discourages. Instead, we might see his view as one of cooperating with providence, doing our part in God's plan.

For the greater glory of God our Lord, our main purpose during this stay at Trent is, while trying to live together in some decent place, to preach, hear confessions, and give lectures while teaching children, giving good example, visiting the poor in hospitals, and exhorting our neighbors—according as each one possesses this or that talent for moving all the persons we can to devotion and prayer, so that they and we may all implore God our Lord that his Divine Majesty will deign to infuse his divine Spirit into all those handling the matters of this high assembly, so that the Holy Spirit may descend upon the council with a greater abundance of gifts and graces.[3]

LETTER TO THE FATHERS OF THE COUNCIL OF TRENT

Of course divine Providence can often guide our actions without our knowing it, and even better than we could imagine or hope; yet it is clear that Providence wishes us to do all that we can on our part and then to trust in its unfailing help."[4]

LETTER TO THE ENTIRE SOCIETY

Suggestions for Further Reading ☐

Barry, William. *Finding God in All Things: A Companion to the Spiritual Exercises of Saint Ignatius.* Notre Dame, IN: Ave Maria Press, 2009.

Fagin, Gerald M. *Putting On the Heart of Christ: How the Spiritual Exercises Invite Us to a Virtuous Life.* Chicago: Loyola Press, 2010.

Fleming, David L. *What Is Ignatian Spirituality?* Chicago: Loyola Press, 2008.

Houdek, Frank. *Guided by the Spirit: A Jesuit Perspective on Spiritual Direction.* Chicago: Loyola Press, 1996.

An Ignatian Spirituality Reader. George Traub, ed. Chicago: Loyola Press, 2008.

Ignatius of Loyola: Letters and Instructions. Martin E. Palmer, John W. Padberg, and John L. McCarthy, eds. St. Louis, MO: The Institute of Jesuit Sources, 2006.

Manney, Tim. *A Simple Life-Changing Prayer: Discover the Power of St. Ignatius Loyola's Examen.* Chicago: Loyola Press, 2011.

Martin, James. *The Jesuit Guide to (Almost) Everything: A Spirituality for Real Life.* New York: HarperOne, 2010.

Mossa, Mark. *Already There: Letting God Find You.* Cincinnati: Saint Anthony Messenger Press, 2010.

Muldoon, Tim. *The Ignatian Workout: Daily Spiritual Exercises for a Healthy Faith.* Chicago: Loyola Press, 2004.

O'Brien, Kevin. *The Ignatian Adventure: Experiencing the Spiritual Exercises of St. Ignatius in Daily Life.* Chicago: Loyola Press, 2011.

A Pilgrim's Testament: The Memoirs of St. Ignatius of Loyola. Parmananda R. Divarkar, trans. St. Louis, MO: The Institute of Jesuit Sources, 1995.

Remembering Iñigo: Glimpses of the Life of Saint Ignatius of Loyola. Alexander Eaglestone & Joseph A. Munitiz, ed. and trans. St. Louis, MO: The Institute of Jesuit Sources, 2004.

Silf, Margaret. *Inner Compass: An Invitation to Ignatian Spirituality.* Chicago: Loyola Press, 2007.

The Spiritual Exercises of St. Ignatius: Based on Studies in the Language of the Autograph. Louis Puhl, trans. and ed. Chicago: Loyola Press, 1968.

Thibodeaux, Mark E. *God's Voice Within: The Ignatian Way to Discover God's Will.* Chicago: Loyola Press, 2010.

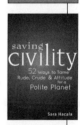
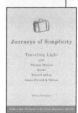

Judaism / Christianity / Islam / Interfaith

All Politics Is Religious: Speaking Faith to the Media, Policy Makers and Community *By Rabbi Dennis S. Ross; Foreword by Rev. Barry W. Lynn*
Provides ideas and strategies for expressing a clear, forceful and progressive religious point of view that is all too often overlooked and under-represented in public discourse. 6 x 9, 192 pp, Quality PB, 978-1-59473-374-1 **$18.99**

Religion Gone Astray: What We Found at the Heart of Interfaith
By Pastor Don Mackenzie, Rabbi Ted Falcon and Imam Jamal Rahman
Welcome to the deeper dimensions of interfaith dialogue—exploring that which divides us personally, spiritually and institutionally.
6 x 9, 192 pp, Quality PB, 978-1-59473-317-8 **$16.99**

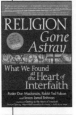

Getting to the Heart of Interfaith: The Eye-Opening, Hope-Filled Friendship of a Pastor, a Rabbi & an Imam *by Pastor Don Mackenzie, Rabbi Ted Falcon and Imam Jamal Rahman*
6 x 9, 192 pp, Quality PB, 978-1-59473-263-8 **$16.99**

Hearing the Call across Traditions: Readings on Faith and Service
Edited by Adam Davis; Foreword by Eboo Patel
6 x 9, 352 pp, Quality PB, 978-1-59473-303-1 **$18.99**; HC, 978-1-59473-264-5 **$29.99**

How to Do Good & Avoid Evil: A Global Ethic from the Sources of Judaism
by Hans Küng and Rabbi Walter Homolka; Translated by Rev. Dr. John Bowden
6 x 9, 224 pp, HC, 978-1-59473-255-3 **$19.99**

Blessed Relief: What Christians Can Learn from Buddhists about Suffering
by Gordon Peerman 6 x 9, 208 pp, Quality PB, 978-1-59473-252-2 **$16.99**

Christians & Jews—Faith to Faith: Tragic History, Promising Present, Fragile Future *by Rabbi James Rudin* 6 x 9, 288 pp, HC, 978-1-58023-432-0 **$24.99***

Christians & Jews in Dialogue: Learning in the Presence of the Other *by Mary C. Boys and Sara S. Lee; Foreword by Dorothy C. Bass* 6 x 9, 240 pp, Quality PB, 978-1-59473-254-6 **$18.99**

InterActive Faith: The Essential Interreligious Community-Building Handbook
Edited by Rev. Bud Heckman with Rori Picker Neiss; Foreword by Rev. Dirk Ficca
6 x 9, 304 pp, Quality PB, 978-1-59473-273-7 **$16.99**; HC, 978-1-59473-237-9 **$29.99**

The Jewish Approach to God: A Brief Introduction for Christians
by Rabbi Neil Gillman, PhD 5½ x 8½, 192 pp, Quality PB, 978-1-58023-190-9 **$16.95***

The Jewish Approach to Repairing the World (*Tikkun Olam*): A Brief Introduction for Christians *by Rabbi Elliot N. Dorff, PhD, with Rev. Cory Willson*
5½ x 8½, 256 pp, Quality PB, 978-1-58023-349-1 **$16.99***

The Jewish Connection to Israel, the Promised Land: A Brief Introduction for Christians *by Rabbi Eugene Korn, PhD* 5½ x 8½, 192 pp, Quality PB, 978-1-58023-318-7 **$14.99***

Jewish Holidays: A Brief Introduction for Christians *by Rabbi Kerry M. Olitzky and Rabbi Daniel Judson* 5½ x 8½, 176 pp, Quality PB, 978-1-58023-302-6 **$16.99***

Jewish Ritual: A Brief Introduction for Christians
by Rabbi Kerry M. Olitzky and Rabbi Daniel Judson 5½ x 8½, 144 pp, Quality PB, 978-1-58023-210-4 **$14.99***

Jewish Spirituality: A Brief Introduction for Christians *by Rabbi Lawrence Kushner*
5½ x 8½, 112 pp, Quality PB, 978-1-58023-150-3 **$12.95***

A Jewish Understanding of the New Testament *by Rabbi Samuel Sandmel;*
New preface by Rabbi David Sandmel 5½ x 8½, 368 pp, Quality PB, 978-1-59473-048-1 **$19.99***

Modern Jews Engage the New Testament: Enhancing Jewish Well-Being in a Christian Environment *by Rabbi Michael J. Cook, PhD* 6 x 9, 416 pp, HC, 978-1-58023-313-2 **$29.99***

Talking about God: Exploring the Meaning of Religious Life with Kierkegaard, Buber, Tillich and Heschel *by Daniel F. Polish, PhD* 6 x 9, 160 pp, Quality PB, 978-1-59473-272-0 **$16.99**

We Jews and Jesus: Exploring Theological Differences for Mutual Understanding
by Rabbi Samuel Sandmel; New preface by Rabbi David Sandmel
6 x 9, 192 pp, Quality PB, 978-1-59473-208-9 **$16.99**

Who Are the *Real* Chosen People? The Meaning of Chosenness in Judaism, Christianity and Islam *by Reuven Firestone, PhD*
6 x 9, 176 pp, Quality PB, 978-1-59473-290-4 **$16.99**; HC, 978-1-59473-248-5 **$21.99**

* A book from Jewish Lights, SkyLight Paths' sister imprint

Sacred Texts—SkyLight Illuminations Series

Offers today's spiritual seeker an enjoyable entry into the great classic texts of the world's spiritual traditions. Each classic is presented in an accessible translation, with facing pages of guided commentary from experts, giving you the keys you need to understand the history, context and meaning of the text.

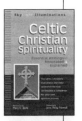

CHRISTIANITY

Celtic Christian Spirituality: Essential Writings—Annotated & Explained
Annotation by Mary C. Earle; Foreword by John Philip Newell
Explores how the writings of this lively tradition embody the gospel.
5½ x 8½, 176 pp, Quality PB, 978-1-59473-302-4 **$16.99**

Desert Fathers and Mothers: Early Christian Wisdom Sayings—
Annotated & Explained
Annotation by Christine Valters Paintner, PhD
Opens up wisdom of the desert fathers and mothers for readers with no previous knowledge of Western monasticism and early Christianity.
5½ x 8½, 176 pp (est), Quality PB, 978-1-59473-373-4 **$16.99**

The End of Days: Essential Selections from Apocalyptic Texts—
Annotated & Explained
Annotation by Robert G. Clouse, PhD
Helps you understand the complex Christian visions of the end of the world.
5½ x 8½, 224 pp, Quality PB, 978-1-59473-170-9 **$16.99**

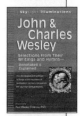

The Hidden Gospel of Matthew: Annotated & Explained
Translation & Annotation by Ron Miller
Discover the words and events that have the strongest connection to the historical Jesus.
5½ x 8½, 272 pp, Quality PB, 978-1-59473-038-2 **$16.99**

The Infancy Gospels of Jesus: Apocryphal Tales from the Childhoods of Mary and Jesus—Annotated & Explained
Translation & Annotation by Stevan Davies; Foreword by A. Edward Siecienski, PhD
A startling presentation of the early lives of Mary, Jesus and other biblical figures that will amuse and surprise you.
5½ x 8½, 176 pp, Quality PB, 978-1-59473-258-4 **$16.99**

John & Charles Wesley: Selections from Their Writings and Hymns—
Annotated & Explained
Annotation by Paul W. Chilcote, PhD
A unique presentation of the writings of these two inspiring brothers brings together some of the most essential material from their large corpus of work.
5½ x 8½, 288 pp, Quality PB, 978-1-59473-309-3 **$16.99**

The Lost Sayings of Jesus: Teachings from Ancient Christian, Jewish, Gnostic and Islamic Sources—Annotated & Explained
Translation & Annotation by Andrew Phillip Smith; Foreword by Stephan A. Hoeller
This collection of more than three hundred sayings depicts Jesus as a Wisdom teacher who speaks to people of all faiths as a mystic and spiritual master.
5½ x 8½, 240 pp, Quality PB, 978-1-59473-172-3 **$16.99**

Philokalia: The Eastern Christian Spiritual Texts—Selections
Annotated & Explained *Annotation by Allyne Smith; Translation by G. E. H. Palmer, Phillip Sherrard and Bishop Kallistos Ware*
The first approachable introduction to the wisdom of the Philokalia, the classic text of Eastern Christian spirituality.
5½ x 8½, 240 pp, Quality PB, 978-1-59473-103-7 **$16.99**

The Sacred Writings of Paul: Selections Annotated & Explained
Translation & Annotation by Ron Miller
Leads you into the exciting immediacy of Paul's teachings.
5½ x 8½, 224 pp, Quality PB, 978-1-59473-213-3 **$16.99**

Sacred Texts—continued

CHRISTIANITY—continued

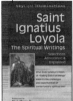

Saint Augustine of Hippo: Selections from *Confessions* and Other Essential Writings—Annotated & Explained
Annotation by Joseph T. Kelley, PhD; Translation by the Augustinian Heritage Institute
Provides insight into the mind and heart of this foundational Christian figure.
5½ x 8½, 272 pp, Quality PB, 978-1-59473-282-9 **$16.99**

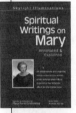

Saint Ignatius Loyola—The Spiritual Writings:
Selections Annotated & Explained *Annotation by Mark Mossa, SJ*
Draws from contemporary translations of original texts focusing on the practical mysticism of Ignatius of Loyola.
5½ x 8½, 288 pp, Quality PB, 978-1-59473-301-7 **$18.99**

Sex Texts from the Bible: Selections Annotated & Explained
Translation & Annotation by Teresa J. Hornsby; Foreword by Amy-Jill Levine
Demystifies the Bible's ideas on gender roles, marriage, sexual orientation, virginity, lust and sexual pleasure.
5½ x 8½, 208 pp, Quality PB, 978-1-59473-217-1 **$16.99**

Spiritual Writings on Mary: Annotated & Explained
Annotation by Mary Ford-Grabowsky; Foreword by Andrew Harvey
Examines the role of Mary, the mother of Jesus, as a source of inspiration in history and in life today.
5½ x 8½, 288 pp, Quality PB, 978-1-59473-001-6 **$16.99**

The Way of a Pilgrim: The Jesus Prayer Journey—Annotated & Explained
Translation & Annotation by Gleb Pokrovsky; Foreword by Andrew Harvey
A classic of Russian Orthodox spirituality.
5½ x 8½, 160 pp, Illus., Quality PB, 978-1-893361-31-7 **$14.95**

JUDAISM

The Book of Job: Annotated & Explained
Translation and Annotation by Donald Kraus; Foreword by Dr. Marc Brettler
Clarifies for today's readers what Job is, how to overcome difficulties in the text, and what it may mean for us.
5½ x 8½, 220 pp (est), Quality PB, 978-1-59473-389-5 **$16.99**

The Divine Feminine in Biblical Wisdom Literature
Selections Annotated & Explained
Translation & Annotation by Rabbi Rami Shapiro; Foreword by Rev. Cynthia Bourgeault, PhD
Uses the Hebrew Bible and Wisdom literature to explain Sophia's way of wisdom and illustrate Her creative energy.
5½ x 8½, 240 pp, Quality PB, 978-1-59473-109-9 **$16.99**

Ecclesiastes: Annotated & Explained
Translation & Annotation by Rabbi Rami Shapiro; Foreword by Rev. Barbara Cawthorne Crafton
A timeless teaching on living well amid uncertainty and insecurity.
5½ x 8½, 160 pp, Quality PB, 978-1-59473-287-4 **$16.99**

Maimonides—Essential Teachings on Jewish Faith & Ethics
The Book of Knowledge & the Thirteen Principles of Faith—Annotated & Explained
Translation and Annotation by Rabbi Marc D. Angel, PhD
Opens up for us Maimonides's views on the nature of God, providence, prophecy, free will, human nature, repentance and more.
5½ x 8½, 224 pp, Quality PB, 978-1-59473-311-6 **$18.99**

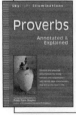

Proverbs: Annotated & Explained
Translation and Annotation by Rabbi Rami Shapiro
Demonstrates how these complex poetic forms are actually straightforward instructions to live simply, without rationalizations and excuses.
5½ x 8½, 288 pp, Quality PB, 978-1-59473-310-9 $16.99

Sacred Texts—continued

ISLAM

Ghazali on the Principles of Islamic Spirituality
Selections from *The Forty Foundations of Religion*—Annotated & Explained
Translation & Annotation by Aaron Spevack, PhD
Makes the core message of this influential spiritual master relevant to anyone seeking a balanced understanding of Islam.
5½ x 8½, 338 pp, Quality PB, 978-1-59473-284-3 **$18.99**

The Qur'an and Sayings of Prophet Muhammad
Selections Annotated & Explained
Annotation by Sohaib N. Sultan; Translation by Yusuf Ali, Revised by Sohaib N. Sultan; Foreword by Jane I. Smith
Presents the foundational wisdom of Islam in an easy-to-use format.
5½ x 8½, 256 pp, Quality PB, 978-1-59473-222-5 **$16.99**

Rumi and Islam: Selections from His Stories, Poems, and Discourses—
Annotated & Explained *Translation & Annotation by Ibrahim Gamard*
Focuses on Rumi's place within the Sufi tradition of Islam, providing insight into the mystical side of the religion.
5½ x 8½, 240 pp, Quality PB, 978-1-59473-002-3 **$18.99**

EASTERN RELIGIONS

The Art of War—Spirituality for Conflict: Annotated & Explained
by Sun Tzu; Annotation by Thomas Huynh; Translation by Thomas Huynh and the Editors at Sonshi.com; Foreword by Marc Benioff; Preface by Thomas Cleary
Highlights principles that encourage a perceptive and spiritual approach to conflict.
5½ x 8½, 256 pp, Quality PB, 978-1-59473-244-7 **$16.99**

Bhagavad Gita: Annotated & Explained
Translation by Shri Purohit Swami; Annotation by Kendra Crossen Burroughs; Foreword by Andrew Harvey
Presents the classic text's teachings—with no previous knowledge of Hinduism required.
5½ x 8½, 192 pp, Quality PB, 978-1-893361-28-7 **$16.95**

Chuang-tzu: The Tao of Perfect Happiness—Selections Annotated & Explained
Translation & Annotation by Livia Kohn, PhD
Presents Taoism's central message of reverence for the "Way" of the natural world.
5½ x 8½, 240 pp, Quality PB, 978-1-59473-296-6 **$16.99**

Confucius, the *Analects:* The Path of the Sage—Selections Annotated
& Explained *Annotation by Rodney L. Taylor, PhD; Translation by James Legge, Revised by Rodney L. Taylor, PhD* Explores the ethical and spiritual meaning behind the Confucian way of learning and self-cultivation.
5½ x 8½, 192 pp, Quality PB, 978-1-59473-306-2 **$16.99**

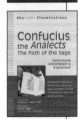

Dhammapada: Annotated & Explained
Translation by Max Müller, revised by Jack Maguire; Annotation by Jack Maguire; Foreword by Andrew Harvey Contains all of Buddhism's key teachings, plus commentary that explains all the names, terms and references.
5½ x 8½, 160 pp, b/w photos, Quality PB, 978-1-893361-42-3 **$14.95**

Selections from the Gospel of Sri Ramakrishna: Annotated & Explained
Translation by Swami Nikhilananda; Annotation by Kendra Crossen Burroughs; Foreword by Andrew Harvey Introduces the fascinating world of the Indian mystic and the universal appeal of his message.
5½ x 8½, 240 pp, b/w photos, Quality PB, 978-1-893361-46-1 **$16.95**

Tao Te Ching: Annotated & Explained
Translation & Annotation by Derek Lin; Foreword by Lama Surya Das
Introduces an Eastern classic in an accessible, poetic and completely original way.
5½ x 8½, 208 pp, Quality PB, 978-1-59473-204-1 **$16.99**

Spirituality

Gathering at God's Table: The Meaning of Mission in the Feast of Faith
By Katharine Jefferts Schori
A profound reminder of our role in the larger frame of God's dream for a restored and reconciled world. 6 x 9, 256 pp, HC, 978-1-59473-316-1 **$21.99**

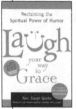

The Heartbeat of God: Finding the Sacred in the Middle of Everything
by Katharine Jefferts Schori; Foreword by Joan Chittister, OSB
Explores our connections to other people, to other nations and with the environment through the lens of faith. 6 x 9, 240 pp, HC, 978-1-59473-292-8 **$21.99**

A Dangerous Dozen: Twelve Christians Who Threatened the Status Quo but Taught Us to Live Like Jesus
by the Rev. Canon C. K. Robertson, PhD; Foreword by Archbishop Desmond Tutu
Profiles twelve visionary men and women who challenged society and showed the world a different way of living. 6 x 9, 208 pp, Quality PB, 978-1-59473-298-0 **$16.99**

Decision Making & Spiritual Discernment: The Sacred Art of Finding Your Way *by Nancy L. Bieber*
Presents three essential aspects of Spirit-led decision making: willingness, attentiveness and responsiveness. 5½ x 8½, 208 pp, Quality PB, 978-1-59473-289-8 **$16.99**

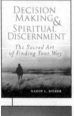

Laugh Your Way to Grace: Reclaiming the Spiritual Power of Humor
by Rev. Susan Sparks A powerful, humorous case for laughter as a spiritual, healing path. 6 x 9, 176 pp, Quality PB, 978-1-59473-280-5 **$16.99**

Bread, Body, Spirit: Finding the Sacred in Food
Edited and with Introductions by Alice Peck 6 x 9, 224 pp, Quality PB, 978-1-59473-242-3 **$19.99**

Claiming Earth as Common Ground: The Ecological Crisis through the Lens of Faith
by Andrea Cohen-Kiener; Foreword by Rev. Sally Bingham
6 x 9, 192 pp, Quality PB, 978-1-59473-261-4 **$16.99**

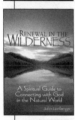

Creating a Spiritual Retirement: A Guide to the Unseen Possibilities in Our Lives
by Molly Srode 6 x 9, 208 pp, b/w photos, Quality PB, 978-1-59473-050-4 **$14.99**

Creative Aging: Rethinking Retirement and Non-Retirement in a Changing World
by Marjory Zoet Bankson 6 x 9, 160 pp, Quality PB, 978-1-59473-281-2 **$16.99**

Keeping Spiritual Balance as We Grow Older: More than 65 Creative Ways to Use Purpose, Prayer, and the Power of Spirit to Build a Meaningful Retirement
by Molly and Bernie Srode 8 x 8, 224 pp, Quality PB, 978-1-59473-042-9 **$16.99**

Hearing the Call across Traditions: Readings on Faith and Service
Edited by Adam Davis; Foreword by Eboo Patel
6 x 9, 352 pp, Quality PB, 978-1-59473-303-1 **$18.99**; HC, 978-1-59473-264-5 **$29.99**

Honoring Motherhood: Prayers, Ceremonies & Blessings
Edited and with Introductions by Lynn L. Caruso
5 x 7¼, 272 pp, Quality PB, 978-1-59473-384-0 **$9.99**

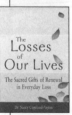

The Losses of Our Lives: The Sacred Gifts of Renewal in Everyday Loss
by Dr. Nancy Copeland-Payton 6 x 9, 192 pp, HC, 978-1-59473-271-3 **$19.99**

Renewal in the Wilderness: A Spiritual Guide to Connecting with God in the Natural World *by John Lionberger*
6 x 9, 176 pp, b/w photos, Quality PB, 978-1-59473-219-5 **$16.99**

Soul Fire: Accessing Your Creativity
by Thomas Ryan, CSP 6 x 9, 160 pp, Quality PB, 978-1-59473-243-0 **$16.99**

A Spirituality for Brokenness: Discovering Your Deepest Self in Difficult Times
by Terry Taylor 6 x 9, 176 pp, Quality PB, 978-1-59473-229-4 **$16.99**

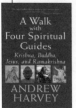

A Walk with Four Spiritual Guides: Krishna, Buddha, Jesus, and Ramakrishna
by Andrew Harvey 5½ x 8½, 192 pp, b/w photos & illus., Quality PB, 978-1-59473-138-9 **$15.99**

The Workplace and Spirituality: New Perspectives on Research and Practice
Edited by Dr. Joan Marques, Dr. Satinder Dhiman and Dr. Richard King
6 x 9, 256 pp, HC, 978-1-59473-260-7 **$29.99**

Spiritual Practice

Fly-Fishing—The Sacred Art: Casting a Fly as a Spiritual Practice
by Rabbi Eric Eisenkramer and Rev. Michael Attas, MD; Foreword by Chris Wood, CEO,
Trout Unlimited; Preface by Lori Simon, executive director, Casting for Recovery
Shares what fly-fishing can teach you about reflection, awe and wonder; the benefits of solitude; the blessing of community and the search for the Divine.
5½ x 8½, 160 pp, Quality PB, 978-1-59473-299-7 **$16.99**

Lectio Divina—**The Sacred Art:** Transforming Words & Images into
Heart-Centered Prayer *by Christine Valters Paintner, PhD*
Expands the practice of sacred reading beyond scriptural texts and makes it accessible in contemporary life. 5½ x 8½, 240 pp, Quality PB, 978-1-59473-300-0 **$16.99**

Writing—The Sacred Art: Beyond the Page to Spiritual Practice
By Rami Shapiro and Aaron Shapiro
Push your writing through the trite and the boring to something fresh, something transformative. Includes over fifty unique, practical exercises.
5½ x 8½, 192 pp, Quality PB, 978-1-59473-372-7 **$16.99**

Dance—The Sacred Art: The Joy of Movement as a Spiritual Practice
by Cynthia Winton-Henry 5½ x 8½, 224 pp, Quality PB, 978-1-59473-268-3 **$16.99**

Everyday Herbs in Spiritual Life: A Guide to Many Practices
by Michael J. Caduto; Foreword by Rosemary Gladstar
7 x 9, 208 pp, 20+ b/w illus., Quality PB, 978-1-59473-174-7 **$16.99**

Giving—The Sacred Art: Creating a Lifestyle of Generosity
by Lauren Tyler Wright 5½ x 8½, 208 pp, Quality PB, 978-1-59473-224-9 **$16.99**

Haiku—The Sacred Art: A Spiritual Practice in Three Lines
by Margaret D. McGee 5½ x 8½, 192 pp, Quality PB, 978-1-59473-269-0 **$16.99**

Hospitality—The Sacred Art: Discovering the Hidden Spiritual Power of Invitation
and Welcome *by Rev. Nanette Sawyer; Foreword by Rev. Dirk Ficca*
5½ x 8½, 208 pp, Quality PB, 978-1-59473-228-7 **$16.99**

Labyrinths from the Outside In: Walking to Spiritual Insight—A Beginner's Guide
by Donna Schaper and Carole Ann Camp
6 x 9, 208 pp, b/w illus. and photos, Quality PB, 978-1-893361-18-8 **$16.95**

Practicing the Sacred Art of Listening: A Guide to Enrich Your Relationships
and Kindle Your Spiritual Life *by Kay Lindahl* 8 x 8, 176 pp, Quality PB, 978-1-893361-85-0 **$16.95**

Recovery—The Sacred Art: The Twelve Steps as Spiritual Practice *by Rami Shapiro;*
Foreword by Joan Borysenko, PhD 5½ x 8½, 240 pp, Quality PB, 978-1-59473-259-1 **$16.99**

Running—The Sacred Art: Preparing to Practice *by Dr. Warren A. Kay; Foreword by*
Kristin Armstrong 5½ x 8½, 160 pp, Quality PB, 978-1-59473-227-0 **$16.99**

The Sacred Art of Chant: Preparing to Practice
by Ana Hernández 5½ x 8½, 192 pp, Quality PB, 978-1-59473-036-8 **$15.99**

The Sacred Art of Fasting: Preparing to Practice
by Thomas Ryan, CSP 5½ x 8½, 192 pp, Quality PB, 978-1-59473-078-8 **$15.99**

The Sacred Art of Forgiveness: Forgiving Ourselves and Others through God's Grace
by Marcia Ford 8 x 8, 176 pp, Quality PB, 978-1-59473-175-4 **$18.99**

The Sacred Art of Listening: Forty Reflections for Cultivating a Spiritual Practice
by Kay Lindahl; Illus. by Amy Schnapper 8 x 8, 160 pp, b/w illus., Quality PB, 978-1-893361-44-7 **$16.95**

The Sacred Art of Lovingkindness: Preparing to Practice
by Rabbi Rami Shapiro; Foreword by Marcia Ford 5½ x 8½, 176 pp, Quality PB, 978-1-59473-151-8 **$16.99**

Sacred Attention: A Spiritual Practice for Finding God in the Moment
by Margaret D. McGee 6 x 9, 144 pp, Quality PB, 978-1-59473-291-1 **$16.99**

Soul Fire: Accessing Your Creativity
by Thomas Ryan, CSP 6 x 9, 160 pp, Quality PB, 978-1-59473-243-0 **$16.99**

Spiritual Adventures in the Snow: Skiing & Snowboarding as Renewal for Your Soul
by Dr. Marcia McFee and Rev. Karen Foster; Foreword by Paul Arthur
5½ x 8½, 208 pp, Quality PB, 978-1-59473-270-6 **$16.99**

Thanking & Blessing—The Sacred Art: Spiritual Vitality through Gratefulness
by Jay Marshall, PhD; Foreword by Philip Gulley 5½ x 8½, 176 pp, Quality PB, 978-1-59473-231-7 **$16.99**

Children's Spirituality

Remembering My Grandparent: A Kid's Own Grief Workbook in the Christian Tradition *by Nechama Liss-Levinson, PhD, and Rev. Molly Phinney Baskette, MDiv* 8 x 10, 48 pp, 2-color text, HC, 978-1-59473-212-6 **$16.99** *For ages 7 & up*

Does God Ever Sleep? *by Joan Sauro, CSJ*
A charming nighttime reminder that God is always present in our lives.
10 x 8½, 32 pp, Full-color photos, Quality PB, 978-1-59473-110-5 **$8.99** *For ages 3–6*

Does God Forgive Me? *by August Gold; Full-color photos by Diane Hardy Waller*
Gently shows how God forgives all that we do if we are truly sorry.
10 x 8½, 32 pp, Full-color photos, Quality PB, 978-1-59473-142-6 **$8.99** *For ages 3–6*

God Said Amen *by Sandy Eisenberg Sasso; Full-color illus. by Avi Katz*
A warm and inspiring tale that shows us that we need only reach out to each other to find the answers to our prayers.
9 x 12, 32 pp, Full-color illus., HC, 978-1-58023-080-3 **$16.95*** *For ages 4 & up*

How Does God Listen? *by Kay Lindahl; Full-color photos by Cynthia Maloney*
How do we know when God is listening to us? Children will find the answers to these questions as they engage their senses while the story unfolds, learning how God listens in the wind, waves, clouds, hot chocolate, perfume, our tears and our laughter.
10 x 8½, 32 pp, Full-color photos, Quality PB, 978-1-59473-084-9 **$8.99** *For ages 3–6*

In God's Hands *by Lawrence Kushner and Gary Schmidt; Full-color illus. by Matthew J. Baek*
9 x 12, 32 pp, Full-color illus., HC, 978-1-58023-224-1 **$16.99*** *For ages 5 & up*

In God's Name *by Sandy Eisenberg Sasso; Full-color illus. by Phoebe Stone*
Like an ancient myth in its poetic text and vibrant illustrations, this award-winning modern fable about the search for God's name celebrates the diversity and, at the same time, the unity of all the people of the world.
9 x 12, 32 pp, Full-color illus., HC, 978-1-879045-26-2 **$16.99*** *For ages 4 & up*

Also available in Spanish: **El nombre de Dios**
9 x 12, 32 pp, Full-color illus., HC, 978-1-893361-63-8 **$16.95**

In Our Image: God's First Creatures
by Nancy Sohn Swartz; Full-color illus. by Melanie Hall
A playful new twist on the Genesis story—from the perspective of the animals. Celebrates the interconnectedness of nature and the harmony of all living things.
9 x 12, 32 pp, Full-color illus., HC, 978-1-879045-99-6 **$16.95*** *For ages 4 & up*

Noah's Wife: The Story of Naamah
by Sandy Eisenberg Sasso; Full-color illus. by Bethanne Andersen
Opens young readers' religious imaginations to new ideas about the well-known story of the Flood. When God tells Noah to bring the animals of the world onto the ark, God also calls on Naamah, Noah's wife, to save each plant on Earth.
9 x 12, 32 pp, Full-color illus., HC, 978-1-58023-134-3 **$16.95*** *For ages 4 & up*

Also available: **Naamah:** Noah's Wife (A Board Book)
by Sandy Eisenberg Sasso; Full-color illus. by Bethanne Andersen
5 x 5, 24 pp, Full-color illus., Board Book, 978-1-893361-56-0 **$7.95** *For ages 0–4*

Where Does God Live? *by August Gold and Matthew J. Perlman*
Helps children and their parents find God in the world around us with simple, practical examples children can relate to.
10 x 8½, 32 pp, Full-color photos, Quality PB, 978-1-893361-39-3 **$8.99** *For ages 3–6*

* A book from Jewish Lights, SkyLight Paths' sister imprint

Spiritual Poetry—The Mystic Poets

Experience these mystic poets as you never have before. Each beautiful, compact book includes a brief introduction to the poet's time and place, a summary of the major themes of the poet's mysticism and religious tradition, essential selections from the poet's most important works, and an appreciative preface by a contemporary spiritual writer.

Hafiz
The Mystic Poets
Translated and with Notes by Gertrude Bell
Preface by Ibrahim Gamard

Hafiz is known throughout the world as Persia's greatest poet, with sales of his poems in Iran today only surpassed by those of the Qur'an itself. His probing and joyful verse speaks to people from all backgrounds who long to taste and feel divine love and experience harmony with all living things.

5 x 7¼, 144 pp, HC, 978-1-59473-009-2 **$16.99**

Hopkins
The Mystic Poets
Preface by Rev. Thomas Ryan, CSP

Gerard Manley Hopkins, Christian mystical poet, is beloved for his use of fresh language and startling metaphors to describe the world around him. Although his verse is lovely, beneath the surface lies a searching soul, wrestling with and yearning for God.

5 x 7¼, 112 pp, HC, 978-1-59473-010-8 **$16.99**

Tagore
The Mystic Poets
Preface by Swami Adiswarananda

Rabindranath Tagore is often considered the Shakespeare of modern India. A great mystic, Tagore was the teacher of W. B. Yeats and Robert Frost, the close friend of Albert Einstein and Mahatma Gandhi, and the winner of the Nobel Prize for Literature. This beautiful sampling of Tagore's two most important works, *The Gardener* and *Gitanjali,* offers a glimpse into his spiritual vision that has inspired people around the world.

5 x 7¼, 144 pp, HC, 978-1-59473-008-5 **$16.99**

Whitman
The Mystic Poets
Preface by Gary David Comstock

Walt Whitman was the most innovative and influential poet of the nineteenth century. This beautiful sampling of Whitman's most important poetry from *Leaves of Grass,* and selections from his prose writings, offers a glimpse into the spiritual side of his most radical themes—love for country, love for others and love of self.

5 x 7¼, 192 pp, HC, 978-1-59473-041-2 **$16.99**

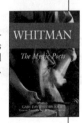

Women's Interest

Women, Spirituality and Transformative Leadership
Where Grace Meets Power
Edited by Kathe Schaaf, Kay Lindahl, Kathleen S. Hurty, PhD, and Reverend Guo Cheen
A dynamic conversation on the power of women's spiritual leadership and its emerging patterns of transformation.
6 x 9, 288 pp, Hardcover, 978-1-59473-313-0 **$24.99**

Spiritually Healthy Divorce: Navigating Disruption with Insight & Hope
by Carolyne Call A spiritual map to help you move through the twists and turns of divorce. 6 x 9, 224 pp, Quality PB, 978-1-59473-288-1 **$16.99**

New Feminist Christianity: Many Voices, Many Views
Edited by Mary E. Hunt and Diann L. Neu
Insights from ministers and theologians, activists and leaders, artists and liturgists who are shaping the future. Taken together, their voices offer a starting point for building new models of religious life and worship.
6 x 9, 384 pp, HC, 978-1-59473-285-0 **$24.99**

New Jewish Feminism: Probing the Past, Forging the Future
Edited by Rabbi Elyse Goldstein; Foreword by Anita Diamant
Looks at the growth and accomplishments of Jewish feminism and what they mean for Jewish women today and tomorrow. Features the voices of women from every area of Jewish life, addressing the important issues that concern Jewish women.
6 x 9, 480 pp, Quality PB, 978-1-58023-448-1 **$19.99**; HC, 978-1-58023-359-0 **$24.99***

Bread, Body, Spirit: Finding the Sacred in Food
Edited and with Introductions by Alice Peck 6 x 9, 224 pp, Quality PB, 978-1-59473-242-3 **$19.99**

Dance—The Sacred Art: The Joy of Movement as a Spiritual Practice
by Cynthia Winton-Henry 5½ x 8½, 224 pp, Quality PB, 978-1-59473-268-3 **$16.99**

Daughters of the Desert: Stories of Remarkable Women from Christian, Jewish and Muslim Traditions
by Claire Rudolf Murphy, Meghan Nuttall Sayres, Mary Cronk Farrell, Sarah Conover and Betsy Wharton
5½ x 8½, 192 pp, Illus., Quality PB, 978-1-59473-106-8 **$14.99** Inc. reader's discussion guide

The Divine Feminine in Biblical Wisdom Literature
Selections Annotated & Explained
Translation & Annotation by Rabbi Rami Shapiro; Foreword by Rev. Cynthia Bourgeault, PhD
5½ x 8½, 240 pp, Quality PB, 978-1-59473-109-9 **$16.99**

Divining the Body: Reclaim the Holiness of Your Physical Self
by Jan Phillips 8 x 8, 256 pp, Quality PB, 978-1-59473-080-1 **$18.99**

Honoring Motherhood: Prayers, Ceremonies & Blessings
Edited and with Introductions by Lynn L. Caruso 5 x 7¼, 272 pp, Quality PB, 978-1-59473-384-0 **$9.99**

Next to Godliness: Finding the Sacred in Housekeeping
Edited by Alice Peck 6 x 9, 224 pp, Quality PB, 978-1-59473-214-0 **$19.99**

ReVisions: Seeing Torah through a Feminist Lens
by Rabbi Elyse Goldstein 5½ x 8½, 224 pp, Quality PB, 978-1-58023-117-6 **$16.95***

The Triumph of Eve & Other Subversive Bible Tales
by Matt Biers-Ariel 5½ x 8½, 192 pp, Quality PB, 978-1-59473-176-1 **$14.99**

White Fire: A Portrait of Women Spiritual Leaders in America
by Malka Drucker; Photos by Gay Block 7 x 10, 320 pp, b/w photos, HC, 978-1-893361-64-5 **$24.95**

Woman Spirit Awakening in Nature: Growing Into the Fullness of Who You Are
by Nancy Barrett Chickerneo, PhD; Foreword by Eileen Fisher
8 x 8, 224 pp, b/w illus., Quality PB, 978-1-59473-250-8 **$16.99**

Women of Color Pray: Voices of Strength, Faith, Healing, Hope and Courage
Edited and with Introductions by Christal M. Jackson
5 x 7¼, 208 pp, Quality PB, 978-1-59473-077-1 **$15.99**

The Women's Torah Commentary: New Insights from Women Rabbis on the 54 Weekly Torah Portions *Edited by Rabbi Elyse Goldstein*
6 x 9, 496 pp, Quality PB, 978-1-58023-370-5 **$19.99**; HC, 978-1-58023-076-6 **$34.95***

* A book from Jewish Lights, SkyLight Paths' sister imprint

Prayer / Meditation

Men Pray: Voices of Strength, Faith, Healing, Hope and Courage
Created by the Editors at SkyLight Paths
Celebrates the rich variety of ways men around the world have called out to the
Divine—with words of joy, praise, gratitude, wonder, petition and even anger—
from the ancient world up to our own day.
5 x 7, 200 pp (est), HC, 978-1-59473-395-6 **$16.99**

Sacred Attention: A Spiritual Practice for Finding God in the Moment
by Margaret D. McGee
Framed on the Christian liturgical year, this inspiring guide explores ways to
develop a practice of attention as a means of talking—and listening—to God.
6 x 9, 144 pp, Quality PB, 978-1-59473-291-1 **$16.99**

Women of Color Pray: Voices of Strength, Faith, Healing, Hope and Courage
Edited and with Introductions by Christal M. Jackson
Through these prayers, poetry, lyrics, meditations and affirmations, you will
share in the strong and undeniable connection women of color share with God.
5 x 7¼, 208 pp, Quality PB, 978-1-59473-077-1 **$15.99**

The Art of Public Prayer, 2nd Edition: Not for Clergy Only
by Lawrence A. Hoffman, PhD 6 x 9, 288 pp, Quality PB, 978-1-893361-06-5 **$19.99**

A Heart of Stillness: A Complete Guide to Learning the Art of Meditation
by David A. Cooper 5½ x 8½, 272 pp, Quality PB, 978-1-893361-03-4 **$18.99**

Living into Hope: A Call to Spiritual Action for Such a Time as This
by Rev. Dr. Joan Brown Campbell; Foreword by Karen Armstrong
6 x 9, 208 pp, HC, 978-1-59473-283-6 **$21.99**

Meditation without Gurus: A Guide to the Heart of Practice
by Clark Strand 5½ x 8½, 192 pp, Quality PB, 978-1-893361-93-5 **$16.95**

Prayers to an Evolutionary God
by William Cleary; Afterword by Diarmuid O'Murchu
6 x 9, 208 pp, HC, 978-1-59473-006-1 **$21.99**

Praying with Our Hands: 21 Practices of Embodied Prayer from the World's
Spiritual Traditions *by Jon M. Sweeney; Photos by Jennifer J. Wilson; Foreword by Mother Tessa
Bielecki; Afterword by Taitetsu Unno, PhD*
8 x 8, 96 pp, 22 duotone photos, Quality PB, 978-1-893361-16-4 **$16.95**

Secrets of Prayer: A Multifaith Guide to Creating Personal Prayer in Your Life
by Nancy Corcoran, CSJ
6 x 9, 160 pp, Quality PB, 978-1-59473-215-7 **$16.99**

Three Gates to Meditation Practice: A Personal Journey into Sufism, Buddhism,
and Judaism *by David A. Cooper* 5½ x 8½, 240 pp, Quality PB, 978-1-893361-22-5 **$16.95**

Prayer / M. Basil Pennington, OCSO

Finding Grace at the Center, 3rd Edition: The Beginning of
Centering Prayer *with Thomas Keating, OCSO, and Thomas E. Clarke, SJ; Foreword by Rev.
Cynthia Bourgeault, PhD* A practical guide to a simple and beautiful form of medita-
tive prayer. 5 x 7¼, 128 pp, Quality PB, 978-1-59473-182-2 **$12.99**

The Monks of Mount Athos: A Western Monk's Extraordinary
Spiritual Journey on Eastern Holy Ground *Foreword by Archimandrite Dionysios*
Explores the landscape, monastic communities and food of Athos.
6 x 9, 352 pp, Quality PB, 978-1-893361-78-2 **$18.95**

Psalms: A Spiritual Commentary *Illus. by Phillip Ratner*
Reflections on some of the most beloved passages from the Bible's most widely
read book. 6 x 9, 176 pp, 24 full-page b/w illus., Quality PB, 978-1-59473-234-8 **$16.99**

The Song of Songs: A Spiritual Commentary *Illus. by Phillip Ratner*
Explore the Bible's most challenging mystical text.
6 x 9, 160 pp, 14 full-page b/w illus., Quality PB, 978-1-59473-235-5 **$16.99**
HC, 978-1-59473-004-7 **$19.99**

About SKYLIGHT PATHS Publishing

SkyLight Paths Publishing is creating a place where people of different spiritual traditions come together for challenge and inspiration, a place where we can help each other understand the mystery that lies at the heart of our existence.

Through spirituality, our religious beliefs are increasingly becoming a part of our lives—rather than *apart* from our lives. While many of us may be more interested than ever in spiritual growth, we may be less firmly planted in traditional religion. Yet, we do want to deepen our relationship to the sacred, to learn from our own as well as from other faith traditions, and to practice in new ways.

SkyLight Paths sees both believers and seekers as a community that increasingly transcends traditional boundaries of religion and denomination—people wanting to learn from each other, *walking together, finding the way.*

For your information and convenience, at the back of this book we have provided a list of other SkyLight Paths books you might find interesting and useful. They cover the following subjects:

Buddhism / Zen	Global Spiritual	Monasticism
Catholicism	Perspectives	Mysticism
Children's Books	Gnosticism	Poetry
Christianity	Hinduism /	Prayer
Comparative	Vedanta	Religious Etiquette
Religion	Inspiration	Retirement
Current Events	Islam / Sufism	Spiritual Biography
Earth-Based	Judaism	Spiritual Direction
Spirituality	Kabbalah	Spirituality
Enneagram	Meditation	Women's Interest
	Midrash Fiction	Worship

Or phone, fax, mail or e-mail to: SKYLIGHT PATHS Publishing
Sunset Farm Offices, Route 4 • P.O. Box 237 • Woodstock, Vermont 05091
Tel: (802) 457-4000 • Fax: (802) 457-4004 • www.skylightpaths.com
Credit card orders: (800) 962-4544 (8:30AM–5:30PM EST Monday–Friday)
Generous discounts on quantity orders. SATISFACTION GUARANTEED. Prices subject to change.

For more information about each book,
visit our website at www.skylightpaths.com